A CHURCH OF HOUSE CHURCHES

AN ARTICULATED AND APPLIED ECCLESIOLOGY

BY JASON SHEPPERD

A Church of House Churches: An Articulated and Applied Ecclesiology

ISBN: 979-8-9863292-0-8

TABLE OF CONTENTS

INTRODUCTION

I chose a random coffee shop in downtown Houston to do some final whittling on this book. As I sit here writing these words, I'm looking at pastors of three other churches in Houston, who also just happen to be here, without any coordinated intention. We've all said hello, hugged each other, and carried on with our work. I personally know and love each of these guys. I respect their love for Jesus, their commitment to His church, and the way we all respectfully work towards unity in the city. I love and value the churches they are leading, and the hard work for the gospel they are doing.

But, we're each doing church uniquely different. Each of us has our own approach, definitions, and in some cases, methods for how we believe a church should accomplish the mission of Jesus. However, in the end, we each agree that the church is Jesus' church. He started it, He leads it, He builds it. It exists for His purposes, and for His glory. It's for Him, and is empowered by Him.

That said, if Jesus is the originator of His church, is He not also its architect? If He entrusted eternal truths and the power of His gospel to His church, does He have some plans for how His church should be structured, and how His mission through the church should be accomplished? Are there any absolutes that should be present in every church, in all people, place, and time?

I believe there are ecclesiological absolutes that God has gifted His leaders to institute in the churches He has entrusted to them. Furthermore, I believe these absolutes are like ecclesiological DNA threaded throughout Scripture, that reveal the foundational components of Jesus' church.

We see these absolutes throughout Scripture, especially in Acts, and in the letters to the churches. In his book, *Forgotten Ways*, Alan Hirsch writes about these absolutes and refers to them as movements of "apostolic genius." Likewise, when it comes to ecclesiology, I believe there is an "ecclesiological genius" present in patterns, structures, and principles that should be part of every church, every where, for all time.

These absolutes are biblical. They are historical. And they are global.

We see these absolutes in church history, as the church practiced the principles taught by the first century leaders. And we see the turn in church history, where movement slowed, as practices and principles shifted, as the church drifted from its Biblically genius absolutes.

Finally, any serious student of the church should logically conclude that the God who owns creation, designed all of the structure by which the human body, the earth and its ecosystems, and the universe exists surely instituted a design to His most enduring creation, the Church.

With that in mind, together as pastors and students of Jesus' church in the next several pages, we will look at some elements that were prescribed and described to us in the Scriptures God gave us to guide us. We will look at biblical examples of how the church started in a city, and how it supported the spread of the gospel around the globe.

We will discuss how that first century structure progressed beyond Scripture into second century church history. We will see the principles that were protected, and how these practices promulgated the gospel globally.

We will look at the reasons why the rapid multiplication movements of the gospel slowed in the fourth century, and how many of these fourth century adjustments carry on today in the majority of the western church world.

Additionally, we will look at how these early church principles and practices are being carried out today. And we will do a deep dive into a prototype that is building, practicing and pursuing these early church elements.

Finally, we'll talk about what you can do, and possibly should do, in response to what is discovered in the pages to come.

Something big is happening in the world. A shift is happening to return the church to what Jesus had originally intended His church to be. I believe Jesus is pruning and purging His church and preparing her for this cataclysmic shift. And He has used politics and pandemics to accelerate this purification. It's hard. But we love it. Because we love His church. That's why we are here together discovering these absolutes.

Notes of Gratitude:

I am grateful for my wife and kids who understand and celebrate what God has called us to be a part of. I love them deeply and would not want to be on this journey without them.

I'm thankful for the elders at Church Project who love and support me. We share a unique calling, and with me they take their responsibility of oversight of our church very seriously.

I love the relatively small but powerful team God has given Church Project to accomplish His calling. We enjoy each other, and at the same time we work incredibly hard for the sake of Jesus and His church.

I am grateful for our House Church leadership. They love and serve and give and sacrifice. It is under their leadership where all of this ecclesiology is fleshed out into beauty and ministry.

I am grateful for a network of church planters who have grabbed this ecclesiology and planted it in other places. We have a unique understanding and appreciation for one another.

I have been blessed by God with great people to mentor and develop me. They are intentional and committed to me and my growth. Some have been with me for almost 20 years.

I am grateful for some good friends who love me, and believe in me.

In the end, these pages would be nothing more than theories and ideals if it were not for the church God has entrusted to our care. I love Church Project. It's a different kind of love to love a church, one that a pastor understands. It's complex, it's deep, it's beautiful. Our church is full of so many people who really love Jesus and His mission. They love each other. They sacrifice and serve for the calling we have. I love this eternally significant project we are a part of. And I love that we do it together.

A NOTE TO PASTORS

Like every pastor, there are moments I think back on when I knew God was pointing me toward His purpose for my life. It was in college when I sensed God calling me to be a pastor. After wrestling with God for years, I finally obeyed and followed what I sensed Him pushing me toward. I began finding my way, learning, growing, and facing much frustration and discouragement as I attempted to surrender in obedience.

But after almost 20 years as a leader and teaching pastor on various church staffs, I knew I wasn't giving the majority of my time to God's original call on my life. I was making disciples where God placed me, but it felt like I was only doing a small fraction of what God had planned for me. I wondered if I could find a place or position in a church that would resemble the church and calling that I read about in the Scriptures—the thought of that kind of church lit my heart on fire.

I became so discouraged with not fulfilling my calling and passions that I thought about leaving the ministry and going in to the marketplace to try and make a ton of money. Then I could at least support churches and ministries with the money I made.

As a last resort, after years of frustration and desperation, I decided to risk it all, and pursue the conviction of the kind of church God had placed on my heart. I wanted to plant a church that was decentralized, with distributed leadership, that practiced living in diverse discipleship community. To me, it didn't matter if 40 people came (which is where we started), 400, or 4,000—I was going to follow with all I had this conviction and desire to create this kind of church. In all honesty, I didn't think my community was ready for a church like this and it would, like most church starts, not exist for very long.

Our first two years were super slow growth. We were planting a new applied ecclesiology, and it wasn't easily accepted by many. We grew from 40 to about 100 people in year one. In year two, we grew to about 200 people. From years to to four, we grew to close to 1,000 people. In just six years the church grew from 40 people to closer to 2,000 people engaged weekly. Now, roughly 4,000 people gather in one location weekly, and about 8,000-10,000 consider Church Project their church.

We have started or helped start over a dozen churches. We now have about 75 House Churches in our part of the city. And more House Churches have been planted by others in other parts of our city, and other cities by Church Project Network churches. We have pursued directing 50% of our collective giving beyond our walls, and we have directed millions of dollars to church planting and gospel-centered ministries in our city and world. Church Project has hundreds of people leading in intentional, one-on-one discipleship relationships, and this is quickly becoming a disciple making movement.

All of this has happened with no centralized office. No phone number. No receptionist. No office foyer. No mailers. No marketing.

We intentionally didn't read the books everyone was reading, or go to the church growth conferences everyone was attending. They didn't seem to work anyway, since the overwhelming majority of church starts were struggling or ceasing to exist after three to four years. We simply took all of the ecclesiological DNA we found in the Bible over the years, study of church history, global church engagement, and decades of church leadership experience, and synthesized these with practical applications we believed should and could work in any context.

When we started our Sunday gatherings we were in an obscure location with no drive-by visibility. I had actually lived in our area for over 15 years and never knew this warehouse district existed in my community. We did no launch events, no big community awareness promotions. We wanted to see if a church could be planted and disciples be made while only relying on believers who became passionate about Jesus, deeply loved one another, and believed in this type of gathering expression enough to invite their neighbors and friends into this community. That was it.

The name of our church, Church Project, was actually not intended to be our name, but was just the essence of our church from the outset. I gave this temporary identifier to the church at the beginning, as I was searching and praying for the right name. But Church Project became a name synonymous with our church community so quickly, we never had the chance find another name. So, the name "Church Project" stuck. I love that an essence of humility is inherently embedded in our name— we are in pursuit of biblical church, and regularly admit we are not there yet, but we have a clear direction. I sometimes tell our people that they are part of a church community that has no name- just like the early church.

We share a brief ecclesiology weekly in our gatherings. We say weekly that we are a church (and we define that), and that we are a project, "a constant pursuit of becoming what Christ originally intended." I'm writing this book because I really love the church. Church Project ecclesiology has produced simple, and organic systems. Our applied ecclesiology has led to abundant generosity, and surprising growth. This has caused many pastors to spend time with us over the years to learn more about what we are doing and how we do it.

This book is a discussion in applied ecclesiology, with some narrative, and some practical application. I'll simply describe what has worked for us and what has helped other pastors in their churches. As our name connotes, and I easily admit, I don't think we have it all together. We are absolutely an ongoing project. But planting and pastoring this church has been mostly fun, fast, and fruitful. So, I'll share what's happened, humbly praying you'll be encouraged to think more deeply and differently about the church.

Whether you are a church planter, or you pastor an already established church, my hope is that this book inspires and equips you as you consider how to shape a biblically-faithful church. We started Church Project to re-think the typical expression of church that many of us have been exposed to, by returning to the early church as clearly as we could pursue it. I hope reading this book will help you, as a pastor, assess how you are living out your calling in the local church, evaluate what you are perpetuating, and ensure that the practices you create align with Scripture. My hope is that by reading this book you begin to think more critically about the most crucial organism on the planet—the church.

Thanks for loving Jesus, for serving His church, and for feeding His sheep. I'm thankful to be in the trenches with you. I pray you'll be refreshed in the calling we share.

Let's rethink church according to the Scriptures, and return to what Jesus originally intended for it to be.

A SHORT CHURCH PROJECT STORY

I grew up in the church. But I didn't grow up thinking about the church. I never thought about leadership or structure or purpose. I just went to church. And I learned good stuff. And Jesus gratefully grabbed my heart at a young age and I grew to love Him and follow Him. And I started being interested in deeper truths of God, which I later understood to be that my doctrine was forming.

I never took a break from attending or serving in church, or studying the Scriptures. Like many of you, I spent much time in discipleship classes and Sunday School classes and conferences and seminars, all the way through many years of rigorous seminary education. And for all of my church life, college life, seminary life, and even beyond, I never heard the word "ecclesiology." I led in churches, taught theology in church, but never considered my theology of the church.

But as I read my Bible, traveled the world, got to know the global church, and read about the historical church, my heart would burn for the biblical church. I started seeing dissonance and distance between much of Scripture and the historical church and the global church, and the churches I was leading and even learning from.

At some point, this dissonance produced discontent, then finally a disconnect. I'm glad it didn't turn to disillusion, but it could have. I tried to lead my existing church environments toward what I was understanding a biblical expression of church to be, but there was no receptivity, and often resistance. So out of desperation, I started a church to pursue an applied ecclesiology. I wanted to see if the church could apply this theology to its practice.

My dream for Church Project began, in some sense, about 25 years before this church was a reality. I was in college, sitting in my truck, praying to God about my calling to serve Him with my life and leadership within the church. I remember asking God, "If you are calling me to pursue this, please let me be part of what you originally intended the church to be." It took over 20 years of ministry for that prayer to be answered.

I love the churches I've served in the past. The people are precious to me, and I am grateful for the fruit and many relationships that have lasted decades. But for most of my churches (all but one, actually), I was struggling as I was wrestling out the distance between the Scriptures and these church contexts. I served God and the people passionately, made disciples as I could, even though I was wrestling with God about His plan for my life all along the way.

I believe God had many reasons for me to be in those churches for many years. He wanted me to pour out my life there and make disciples. He wanted me to grow and mature. But, He also wanted to use those environments to refine my deeper convictions and give clarity about what church actually is and is not. In doing so He refined my ecclesiology, and created in me an absolute inability to remain in pastoral ministry without rethinking church according to the Scriptures, and re-approaching with a defined ecclesiology.

I was in Malawi, Africa, on a trip to discover how we could meet needs in an area and begin planting the gospel and making disciples through church planting. People came from all over to join us. I remember one lady, I believe they said she was in her 70s (well above the average age for life expectancy there at the time), who I was told walked almost two hours to be with us. They said she had no other gathering of Christ-followers anywhere close to where she lived. As we sang songs to worship Jesus, and taught the Scriptures, I remember thinking, "Could my current church fit here?" The answer of course was, "no." But, I remember wrestling with whether or not it should be able to. Were there any consistent church elements that should be here and there and everywhere?

After many years of student ministry, I became a teaching pastor at a large church—one with great facilities, a large campus, a solid reputation, widespread impact, and thousands of incredible people. God was moving there in great ways, and I had great teams to lead. For years, the church leaders and I had discussed the line of succession I would step into whenever the lead pastor (whom I loved and respected deeply—and still do) would retire. But there was finally a moment when I just said to myself, "I am not intended to keep doing what I am doing."

A final event leading up to my decision to leave and risk everything I had ever known, was time spent meditating on a parable I had known for years—the parable of the talents (Matt. 25:14–30). In this story, Jesus expresses God's frustration with somebody who doesn't fully leverage their opportunity, blessing, and gifting. I wasn't stewarding my gifts and vision and passion and calling, out of a mix of fears and insecurities, and lack of clarity for what forward looked like. I felt an overwhelming sense of conviction that I wasn't properly or fully stewarding my gifts.

God had been developing and teaching me under some good, and more not so good leadership, for many years. But now, I knew it was time. Something deep in my soul, that had held me back all of these years, was gone—it was immediately different. I remember calling my wife and saying, "What I've been wrestling with, the things that have been holding me back, are over. I'm released. I'm done, and I can't lead church in this way anymore."

That's when I decided to risk everything. I had submitted to God's process of preparation for years. I was patiently waiting for Him to cultivate His plans for me, and until this point God had not revealed to me that it was time for me to do this new thing. I went to the lead pastor and respectfully said, "I need to co-pastor, or I need to leave and go pastor. I have to steward my calling in more ways than I am now."

I anticipated this conversation would lead to my amicable departure, with the pastor and church's blessing, but without any financial support or sending. It was, as Bill Hybels called it, "a righteous indignation." It was holy discontent. It was a combination of God finally letting me step into my calling and the fact that I was then 35 years old and sensed, "If not now, when?" It was this sense that there was more to my ministry than what I was currently doing. I literally could not not do it.

Honestly, I didn't even really consider the riskiness of this move. Risk wasn't part of the conversation or consideration. I just knew that I had to try or die trying this thing God had cultivated in my heart; and though I thought might metaphorically die, meaning kill all of the vocational ministry momentum I had built for decades, I was going to give it all I had. It might not work, but the obedience would be worth it. That was it.

If I hadn't taken this step, I would likely have left vocational ministry as a pastor. I had to either take a step into my calling, or I had to walk away entirely, because I knew that what I was perpetuating wasn't the fullness of my calling. It wasn't bad, but it wasn't full. It wasn't full because God had called me, prepared me, and cultivated me for something else.

I wanted to make sure I left with honor in every way. If Jesus was leading me to do something, even something like leave a church, I knew it must be done honorably (the same should be true for every decision in my life). I have seen too many people hurt one church in order to help another. I don't believe this is honoring to God, or His church.

My pastor and I talked about what our relationship would be like going forward. We wanted to be on the same page and clear about our expectations. I assured him I would always support the work of his church, and I wanted to start a new culture and DNA, with new people, in a new place. Likewise he assured me he would continue to support the new work in prayer and personal mentorship. Over time, this would end up being true for both of us. We intentionally continued meeting together monthly to ensure our relationship remained strong. We've since traveled internationally together. We have only ever honored one another.

Calling is more than simply a desire to do something great for God. Calling involves a decision on the part of God that we simply respond to and step into. God anoints pastors for their role. I didn't want to do anything that God wasn't initiating, that didn't originate with Him. I wanted His will, His hand, and His anointing on this.

Anointing is the powerful and present presence of God for His purpose. He calls us and then appoints us for that role. Our response is to receive the calling because it comes from Him. We can request His anointing, but He is not required to give it to us. Once given, we seek to remain in that anointing by living a holy life of obedience, or He may remove the anointing.

I left my position quickly—just a few weeks after the initial conversation with my pastor—and I immediately went to the mountains alone to think and pray. I prayed alone for several days, saying, "God, I have no idea what to do. Although I believe you're in this, I have no idea what direction to take." I had no plans, no church name, no direction, no money, no people—all I had was a compilation of convictions that weren't yet fully clear, and a sense calling.

That week, God gave me my first four steps to take. Those four things were: First, gather some interested people for conversational meetings. I had no idea who those people would be because I knew I would not invite anyone who was a part of my former church. Secondly, start looking for a few guys who would be willing to take this risk with me. I did not yet know anyone who had this in their heart, or who was willing to step into this with me. Thirdly, put together a board of advisors. A group of wise, godly people who would not necessarily be a part of this new church with me, but who could counsel me through the process. Finally, begin looking for a simple place that could be a central gathering space where we might begin sharing and exercising this vision and calling.

The first thing I did when I got back from the mountains was put together a board of advisors who were faithful in my life. They were people who had walked with me through the years and knew my calling. I trusted their relationship with Jesus, their love for the church, and their love for me. They had a wide variety of experience and leadership in different domains. To this day, most have remained a constant source of wisdom, courage and sound counsel.

Then, God crossed my path with several guys who wanted to take a risk serving alongside me. I didn't know two of them beforehand, and the other one was only a casual acquaintance. They had not developed this expression of ecclesiology. But once I shared the vision for Church Project, they wanted to be a part. And I needed help in several arenas.

The four of us started having regular meetings together. I treated them like staff meetings, as if we actually worked together and had a church to lead. We would pray, study the Scriptures, define our roles, create tasks, and make plans together. I held us accountable as a team, and I encouraged them as they encouraged me. We planned and prayed together for four months. We became a team before we had any people, any money, salaries, a place, or even a name.

One month after the mountain trip, we had our first information gathering, and somehow about 40 people came to it. The same number continued to show up to each of the next three information conversations, with about 25 repeat attenders. So, by the time we started, we had somewhere around 25-40 people in our core.

We didn't want to be divisive, so we asked people not to invite anybody to join us from a church where they'd most recently served or attended. We were committed to building unity in our city, and avoiding a sizable migration from another church and a large sharing of former DNA. It was a fresh start—a collection of Christians from all throughout the area—with no certain church represented more than another. It was a melting pot of believers willing to dream together. I knew very few of the people who showed up, but some of the few people I did know are still with us today. In fact, many of these original people have stayed for over a decade.

At those first meetings, we talked about what we saw in the Bible, what the local church should look like based upon what we saw in the Scriptures, and how we could apply those ideas to our place and time. I told these people who were investigating, "I have no idea what a church like this looks like, but we're going to be a group of people who figure it out. I don't know if there'll be 40, 400, or 4,000 people. It really is, in many ways, a project. We're going to see if we can discover this together." And that's what we would do—invite people to join together in a pursuit of what Christ originally intended His church to be.

There was no break between those smaller meetings and our launch as a church. We just started doing church. On our first official Sunday as a church, 1.10.10, 40 people came together to be a part of this pursuit. We divided the 40 into two House Churches. Those two House Churches become four within months. This quickly became the model of ongoing multiplication of House Churches that has allowed for us to expand our House Churches throughout the city. I explain with more detail this process in later chapters.

We had very simple Sunday Gatherings. And everything else you would expect from your "church" was then distributed to the House Church. It was unusual for everyone joining us, including me. We had never been a part of something so simple and decentralized.

Beyond Sundays, people started building community in House Churches. There was nothing else for them to do if they wanted to be a part of this church community. There were no other options or substitutes.

I've heard church planters say, "Let's build a core for a long time, and then we'll start doing Bible studies in a living room and share the vision until people get it." I understand that, and it's not altogether a bad idea. Sometimes, it is the best approach. But almost 80 percent of church plants fail, a failure rate that rivals that of small businesses. With those odds, I would rather start a church using a different approach.

Many church planters are starting church the same way, reading the same books, going to the same conferences, and then wondering why they are getting the same results. But I wanted to try something different, and start the church like I saw Paul starting churches in the Bible. He immediately started doing what he was called to do: preach the Word, and develop and deploy other leaders. My primary gifts are not suitable for leading small groups. I'm really not great at that. I needed to start exercising my primary gifts of teaching and leadership. That was perhaps one of my first big lessons in church planting. If you are considering church planting or you currently lead a church, be aware of how God has designed you for ministry and create a context where you can operate primarily out of those gifts.

God has caused great growth over the years, even though we haven't changed much of anything since the beginning. Our gatherings look the same, our overall church structure is the same. We've never done a mailer, a commercial, or marketing campaign (I'm not saying this is bad, I'm just showing that it's possible to grow through people personally inviting other people). For our first four years, our gatherings met in an obscure warehouse that was set off of the main road. You had to work to find us.

By the end of our first year, about 100 people were part of our church community. By the end of year two, around 200 people were with us. Between years two and four, roughly 1,000 people were joining together. Between years four and six, we had 2,000 people weekly with us. Then, we kept growing, to roughly 4,000 people gathering weekly, and eleven years into this journey, there are 8-10,000 people who call Church Project their church community (post-pandemic). In addition to our weekly in person attendance, tens of thousands of people from all over the world have somehow found our podcast and are listening to it each month.

We had no sending church, and no outside financial support. We started our church with literally about $500 dollars in the bank. Our first-year budget ended up being around $275,000 dollars. By year six or seven, we had a budget between three and four million dollars. As of this writing, it's grown significantly more. We decided early on to radically and sacrificially invest into gospel-centered ministry partnerships and church planting. We have been able to give many millions of dollars to support Gospel-centered efforts well beyond the name and leadership of Church Project. This in addition to the uncounted financial benevolence that happens weekly within House Churches, Church Project has been able to be uniquely philanthropic in our city and world. Our financial approach has also allowed us to partner with 16 Church Project plants, and support other churches not associated with the Church Project Network.

I bring up all of these numbers only to give some proof of concept, a prototype if you will, that it is possible to be a church with distributed leadership, decentralized into diverse community, and still see some phenomenal things happen. We wouldn't encourage anyone to go and do what we've done unless we were sure it would work.

We don't think highly of ourselves. We have simply followed what we have deeply studied in Scripture, depending on the presence and power of the Spirit all along the way. That said, we are still working to figure so many things out. I am more aware of our weaknesses and opportunities to grow than anyone else. This church is God's work. Jesus said He would build His church. And I've seen that principle come to fruition at Church Project.

People sometimes ask me if I'm surprised at what has happened at Church Project in such a short time. I tell them I don't really think about it like that. I'm excited about what's happened, but I'm not satisfied, so I don't feel surprised. Our city is still primarily unreached. Needs are primarily still unmet. Most people in our city don't live in biblical community. Churches need to be planted locally and globally. I'm far from ready to relax. I'm driven and passionate about the dreams He's put in my heart for His church, so I'm always thinking about where He is leading us. I'm no more surprised about our journey than I would have been if the church hadn't made it to this point. It could have easily have gone either way. But God somehow decided to start something and sustain it so He could use us for His purposes.

According to the best church-planting practices and plans, we should be failing. And that may be the point. We've tirelessly sought to mimic Jesus and His methods, and we believe that's where the power lies. Some pastors of the largest churches I know, men I deeply respect and continue to learn from, have told me, "Jason, we love what you are doing and how you operate, we feel like we're stuck and we don't know how to get off the hamster wheel." One successful pastor who has had great influence in my life told me, "If we did this—which I wish we could, and I want to—our church would fall apart." I understand that. It's hard to imagine big change because many of our systems in the church are deeply rooted. We fear we'll lose people, stop progress, or capsize the ministry if we change.

I know the hesitation, but I don't think that's a reason to stay as we are. We have some accountability to be open to seeing more of what God planned for His very own church. When we started, we certainly took a risk, but we believed what we were pursuing was theologically true. That's why we did it. It boils down to this: if the approach is biblical, we are all constrained to follow that biblical expression, and we should have nothing to fear. But that doesn't mean we don't have to take a risk.

My goals for this book are simple. I want to help rethink church according to the Scriptures, and, in light of the evidence found there, scrutinize church practices that don't actually come from Scripture. From there, I hope to give pastors faith and confidence in the Word of God, and trust that the Spirit of God can grow His church best via His ways. Finally, I pray this book helps the church make disciples more effectively so that Jesus is exalted and the gospel is spread.

CHAPTER 1:

BRIEF ARTICULATED ECCLESIOLOGY

All good pastors care about doctrine. Doctrine is the revealed truth of God. And a pastor's and Bible teacher's job is to help people understand truths about God- who God is, how God works, and how we live in relationship to God and His purposes and plans.

The Apostle Paul told Timothy to "watch your life and doctrine closely, because if you do, you will save both yourself and your hearers." Solid doctrine is crucial for a healthy believer and a mature church and an effective mission.

As leaders, we appropriately develop our doctrine of creation, sin, salvation, and the return of Christ. We know how to explain, express, and defend our beliefs about God. We have biblically informed views of creation, the incarnation, the crucifixion, the resurrection, and the return of Christ.

We know that doctrine comes from Scripture. Doctrine can't be built from pre-existing alternative worldviews, or philosophy, or opinion, or preferences. Doctrine is based upon what the Scripture has to say. We build our doctrine based upon a connectivity from the revealed truths of God's Word.

That said, when it comes to the doctrine of the church, most notably ecclesiology, many pastors share an obviously underdeveloped doctrine. We have general ideas of what a church is, and what a church should be doing. But, compared to all other areas of theology, our ecclesiology is lacking.

Most people do not have ecclesiological conversations. Ecclesiology is a hidden topic in theological books, writings, journals, and seminaries. It's rare to find a group of people having public conversations about ecclesiology. You'll be hard pressed to find an ecclesiology conference this year. The church is the carrier of doctrine to God's people. But we are often carrying a tonnage of well developed doctrine in a vessel of underdeveloped ecclesiology.

We would plead with our people to base their belief system not off of past experience or preference, but clearly from the Scriptures. We study, write curriculum, preach sermons, connect in relationships, and invest many conversations with our people to teach them clearly what God's word says, and pray and work toward a complete doctrine in each of their lives.

But in similar ways to our people's preferential or personally developed doctrine, many pastors today are leading their church context based off of past experience, preference or, philosophical ideology of culture and context. Rather, as pastors and elders and leaders within a church, we should have a robust, clear, biblically informed theology of the church. We need a more developed ecclesiology. We need to be able to more fully express and explain, clearly and concisely, from Scripture, with our Bibles open- what is the church, how does it function, and what is its purpose.

The immediate response of many who have been leading in the church for years is indifference to this topic. They're making disciples, working hard, some good stuff is happening, the basics of the church are being accomplished. So…why do I need to rethink or refine this arena of my ecclesiology?

Or, more practically, if rethinking ecclesiology results in some revelation that change must occur in your current context of church leadership, the energy required and the risk involved in this applied ecclesiological adjustment is not worth it.

But, with exceptions for sure, many pastors would have a hard time taking their Bible and explaining from Scripture why they have the leadership structure, processes and systems, programs and budgets in place that they do.

Nothing may need to change in your church context. Your ecclesiology may be refined and complete. Your application of ecclesiology in the structure and systems of your church may be on point. Your teaching on the church may be clear, and your people can articulate, not your vision and mission statements, but the theology of the church.

Since we all care about doctrine, maybe we could be open to consider and reflect upon our current theology of the church. Maybe we would ask God to reveal to us anything from His Word that we should be aware of, accept, and adjust to become more pleasing to Him? Maybe we could all grow just a bit more in our ecclesiology?

In the birth of the first church, God created strands of DNA that should be present in every subsequent body of believers. This DNA was produced and passed down from the first God-created church body, and should be pursued and possessed by every church since the inception of the first.

In our early beginnings at Church Project, we were driven by this question: "What do we see in Scripture about how Jesus designed His church?" We then worked to mimic that answer as closely as possible. The point of this book essentially is to tell you what we saw in Scripture and how we've sought to replicate it.

I've often heard what you may be thinking right now. The message doesn't change, but the methods do. Culture has changed and is different in every place and people. I agree, but only partially.

The launching of the early church immediately represented cultures and colors and customs and people groups from all over the world. The early church was immediately cross-cultural. Yet, it was consistent in its basis and structure. As we look at the Scriptures, we find these same structures in the multi-cultural and multi-national early church. And we see these same elements represented for the first three centuries where the gospel rapidly spread around the globe.

I've traveled all over the world, and some things are always true in every developed and undeveloped nation. People need the church. They long to gather with other believers. There is power in a large, collective gathering of people, and in smaller communities of people knowing each other deeply. People may not have buildings, but in every culture people have some form of home and shelter. And there are always people close who are in need, so there are always opportunities for believers to meet needs in their city and to serve one another.

In the Gospels, we read that everything Jesus did was about making disciples. It's no surprise then that two of His basic and final commands for the apostles were "make disciples" (Matt. 28:18–20) and "feed my sheep" (John 21:17).

This is exactly what Jesus did the entire time He was on earth. He was making disciples when He taught people on the mountainside by the thousands. When He lived life together with people by the dozens and one-on-one, He was making disciples as well. And, He was making disciples when He was meeting the needs of others.

We see that the early church followed in His footsteps. They met inside the temple courts by the thousands. They met regularly in houses across the city by the dozens. They met the various needs of those around them, in their church body, and in the city.

We wanted to pursue what the early church did, and not only what they did, but how they did what they did. We decided to concern ourselves with these three foundational elements present in the structure of the early church: Simple Sunday morning Gatherings of the entire church based on Scriptural teaching, worship, prayer, and giving; connected House Churches of smaller diverse discipleship communities with distributed pastoral leadership, decentralized from priest and place (we will take deeper look at this in the next chapter); and we formed Ministry Partnerships to serve those in need in our city and world. We began to do these things and only these things, and slowly we began to turn the flywheel on these pillars.

Though some similarities are recognizable in many modern churches, there are also significant differences in how the early church did these few and simple things. And, equally as important, so much of what happens today, the early church did not do.

CHAPTER 2

A CHURCH OF HOUSE CHURCHES

Growing up I only attended one kind of church, from birth through college, and many years beyond. Every expression of a group was a Sunday School class, and it happened under one roof. I never thought of anything other than this one way of doing church.

I had some really good Sunday School teachers growing up. They taught me the Bible incredibly well. I grew to love Jesus, and His Word, and the church, and I thank them for their spiritual influence in my life.

I also led in this church context for many years. I perpetuated some good things. But, after experiencing a Church of House Churches, I have realized that I was building into things that were good, but less than what the Word teaches us that the fullness of church should be.

I got "crazy" once and went to work for a church that had small groups. I thought I was rebellious. To some of my mentors, me leaving a Sunday school model and prevailing denominational church for a small group model non-denominational church was equivalent to leaving the faith.

But, these groups in this place didn't function as a House Church, a small church. They were fellowship groups, or discussion groups, or service groups, or whatever else. But they weren't churches. Some of the leaders were mature in their faith. Some were not. But they all had good motives. But none of the leaders were responsible for fully pastoring that community.

I felt that I had moved a step closer to what I was reading about in the Bible. More freedom in the church, a little less centralized, meeting in homes. But, there still seemed to be a huge disconnect between what I was reading about in Scripture, and what was happening in these small groups. So, having groups in homes wasn't the sole catalytic answer I was searching for and wrestling with for years.

Most of my life, I had never heard of House Church. Then, when I started getting out a little bit more, and started reading about what was happening in God's great big kingdom, I started to hear about House Churches.

Surprisingly, most of what I read about from existing leaders in the world of House Churches disappointed me. It seemed that many of their expressions of House Church were retaliations against the large/mega/corporate kind of churches that their commentaries seemed to rail against. Or, there was often an elitist or separatist attitude present, like they were better than the people who went to normal or big churches. But their ecclesiology seemed incomplete and omitted beautiful portions of God's revealed church.

For the majority of my investigation into the existing idea of House Churches, these communities were isolated. And, most of these House Churches didn't grow and multiply. They seemed to be content being together with themselves. I'm sure exceptions existed. But I was looking, and couldn't find connected, multiplying House Churches anywhere.

This not only saddened and confused me for connectivity into the larger body of believers in a city. It also made me curious as to how, or if they intended to, leverage this community of believers to impact their city for the gospel. How did these internally focused and isolated House Churches live on mission if their intent and practice was not to share the gospel and make disciples who would multiply disciples and multiply House Churches. How would they help many people begin following Jesus?

How do you expect to make a dent in meeting the needs of your city if you're content to be an isolated community of a dozen or so people? How, if there's no compelling calling for every disciple to multiply by sharing the gospel and discipling others. I concluded there must be a greater connected body of believers if a church hopes to reach its city with the Gospel and meet its greater needs.

Aside from all of this, in an isolated and independent House Church, how could they expect to have an impact on the unity of the greater body of Christ in the city?

Even with all of this disappointing revelation through my investigation of the existing condition and expression of House Church in the west, I couldn't get away from the reality of House Church in Scripture, church history, and the global church. So, rather than wondering if House Church was part of God's plan for church or not, I had to start asking questions about what House Church was supposed to be like, and what was its purpose and function and connection to and role in the larger church?

When I started Church Project, I had never experienced a House Church. And I had no proof that a church could become a Church of House Churches. But, I longed to see a church that looked like what I read about in the book of Acts. A church where people loved and knew each other so deeply that they would be willing to sell their possessions and give to one another. A church where people would live like a diverse spiritual family in a discipleship community, where everyone would have pastor that knew them and was available to them, and who were connected to other House Churches to impact their city.

For the first couple of years, I didn't actually know if a church like this would make it. It was slow, it was different, and it felt really fragile. But eventually, it began to work, and now I could never go back.

Early on, some people were excited to learn about this expression of church. They would express that this was a longing in their hearts for years, as they studied the Scriptures and loved the church. But sometimes I found resistance from other pastors regarding our approach to church—particularly calling House

Churches "House Churches," and House Church Pastors "House Church Pastors." It was somewhat confounding for me, but I think it had to do with how different this model was for them. And, maybe some people felt threatened giving so much of their leadership away.

Part of the differences were nomenclature. House Church and House Church Pastor were identifiers that didn't seem appropriate to some, likely due to an unexpressed protection of the role of clergy. They feared that applying the word pastor to some doctor, attorney, engineer, fireman, or whoever, might diminish the role of the pastorate. To some, it seemed to delegitimize the sanctity of the role of a pastor.

I remember one meeting where a local pastor sat down with me. (When we were very small, no one seemed to care, notice or wanted to help Church Project.) This pastor, in a frustrated tone, asked what right I had to follow a House Church expression of church when everybody else was doing it another way. Why should we change things from a small group and leader, to a House Church and pastor?

I told him that I was more than willing to discuss our various approaches based on Scripture, but since he seemed to be the one that was upset, that he got to go first. I asked him to describe his approach and methodology using the Bible as a foundation, and then I would do the same. After being unusually silent for a moment, he said, "I can't argue my position, or why yours is wrong, from the Bible. But I still don't feel good about it." I said humbly but confidently, "Okay, I can. Let's open our Bibles. I'll show you from these passages why I believe we should do things this way."

We have a lot of DNA evidence of the construct of the church littered throughout the letters to the churches, and the pastoral letters. One clear place to get a quick picture of distributed pastoral leadership, decentralized into diverse discipleship communities, is Titus chapters 1 and 2. We'll dig more deeply into these Scriptures in the next chapter.

Titus gives us a glimpse of a "Church of House Churches" - one church comprised of many House Churches. Titus was creating many decentralized House Church communities by enlisting, equipping, identifying, and empowering House Church pastors to oversee House Churches all across Crete.

Paul wanted Titus to have DISTRIBUTED pastoral leadership, DECENTRALIZED from priest and place, into pastoring DIVERSE DISCIPLESHIP communities, connected by common elder oversight.

House Churches across Crete were connected under Titus's leadership. They had doctrinal and behavioral and missional accountability, connectivity to one another and to Titus, support for one another, and common purpose. Together, they had a common mission to share the gospel and make disciples across Crete.

Many expressions of individual and isolated House Church lose their power and potential impact in a city by limiting their connectivity to one another. They start with many biblical values that should be represented in a House Church, but due to their lack of connectivity to other House Churches, they often fail to fully accomplish their mission.

On the other hand, many expressions of super-centralized churches lose their power and potential impact by limiting pastoral leadership to primary pastor and primary place. They most often have drastically diminished expressions of truly distributed and empowered pastoral leadership, they live in homogenous not diverse communities, and the priesthood of each believer is not prioritized.

When you have decentralized expressions of diverse discipleship communities with distributed leadership empowered to pastor, and at the same time you maintain some centrality of oversight for training, accountability, support, and shared mission, you have the combustion of potential in the church.

We see this begin in the first century with Paul and those he led. But, did it continue? Insight into the second century gives clarity that this structure of leadership not only held, but was the structure used to carry the movement of the gospel around the world, for millions of people, over the next several centuries.

Unfortunately there does not exist enough insight into first century continuation of practices. But, Michael Kruger, in his book, *"Christianity at the Crossroads: How the Second Century Shaped the Future of the Church,"* gives a clear picture of how the church continued to function beyond the first century.

Kruger writes extensively on the topic of second century church, and on the topic of connectivity of House Churches in a city. I'll provide several paragraphs of insight from him, for you, here:

> *A similar phenomenon seems to be present in the second century. The letter of 1 Clement, for example, writes on behalf of 'the Church of God . . . in Rome' and writes to 'the Church of God . . . in Corinth'. Despite the fact that* **Rome and Corinth are probably composed of numerous house churches,** *the author apparently views them, in some fashion,* **as a single entity.** *The author even refers to the 'presbyters' in Corinth, implying* **that the church there is ruled by a single body of elders.**

> *Likewise, Polycarp writes, 'to the Church of God . . . in Philippi' even though the city, most likely, has* **numerous house-based congregations.** *Thus, there appears to be some awareness that* **multiple congregations in a single locale are somehow linked together.**

> *And Polycarp calls the Philippians to submit to their 'presbyters', implying again that the Philippian church was* **unified under a single ruling body.** *The church governance during the first and early second century provides a possible explanation for how* **churches in a single city were linked together** *in this fashion.*

> *As a church began in a particular city it would have often been small enough to meet in a single house and would have been governed simply by a group of elders/ presbyters. As such congregations grew in numbers and were forced to meet in additional houses, there may have been situations where* **a single group of elders found themselves ruling over multiple congregations** *in different locations throughout the city.*

> *These* **multiple congregations** *would have been naturally connected by the fact that they were* **led by the same group of elders.** *Thus, Christians in a given city, even worshipping in separate house churches, would have been able to maintain*

*some **common identity under the leadership** of a single body of presbyters. In some instances, as discussed above, the multiplicity of house churches in a particular city could have led to a monepiscopate, where a singular bishop would preside over numerous churches in a single locale (e.g., the bishop of Rome)."*

A "Church of House Churches" then is one church composed of many House Churches, overseen by one common group of elders, led by many House Church pastors, sharing mission and vision and support in a city.

One Sunday, a man found his way to one of our Sunday Gatherings. I asked him how he found us, and he told me he had heard of a church in our city comprised of House Churches. I asked him why he was interested in that, and if he had been a part of anything like this before.

He told me that he had been a part of a House Church for many years that met in the restaurant of his House Church pastor. But, their House Church pastor got cancer, and the family had to close their restaurant to move to be closer to family for his treatment. As a result, his House Church that he loved so much dissolved.

I told him that I was very sorry to hear that his House Church pastor had cancer. And, also that his House Church closed down. After showing appropriate pastoral care and concern for his situation I went on to tell him why that scenario would not happen at Church Project.

I told him that our elders would have stepped in to see how we could support him and his family, and possibly even leading his restaurant, for a season. I told him that we would have been helping develop another pastor to succeed this pastor, and the House Church would have continued under new leadership during this season. Or, they could have been grafted into the House Church geographically closest to theirs.

In disconnected or isolated House Church situations, the House Church pastor often has no support, encouragement, or accountability. What happens when the House Church pastor gets discouraged and considers quitting? What happens when the House Church pastor needs development in his pastoral abilities, or theological training, or support in difficult pastoral situations? What happens when the House Church pastor starts stepping into sinful arenas of his life, and has no one to ask him the difficult questions or set up systems for accountability?

In disconnected or isolated House Churches, the answer to these questions is often, no one. But, in a "Church of House Churches," there are elders who oversee House Churches, who can ensure that all of these things are provided for, for the sake of all of the people that we are entrusted to oversee.

There is a beauty in connectivity. The overreach of centralization can be avoided, so there is no need for the overreaction of isolation and disconnectedness other House Churches. We can have a true decentralized House Church community, and still have some centralization for support, development, and synergy.

Most people agree that a major problem of some large centralized churches is a lack of leadership and pastoral accountability. We need accountability and support throughout every level of leadership. Even House Church pastors need accountability and support. As I say, "every pastor needs a pastor."

A "Church of House Churches" can provide training and development for House Church pastors. Most often, when a fireman or doctor or businessperson or teacher or accountant or attorney become a House Church pastor, they feel intimated, and want support, training, accountability, and encouragement. Connected together with oversight, a "Church of House Churches" is able to provide these things.

Occasionally a House Church pastor or host moves, and at that point we have oversight to step in and support to hopefully ensure the continuation of that House Church. Ideally, and usually, that House Church pastor has been preparing the person who will pastor after their departure. On the very rare occurrence where a House Church pastor has been removed, or removed themselves, due to disqualifying sin in their life, collective leadership can step in to care for the House Church and walk them through the transition.

And, every city has unique needs and opportunities for the gospel to be spread and shown. As a "Church of House Churches," there are opportunities to provide powerfully for the needs in a city through collaboration. Due in part to subtle centralization, many House Churches can function as one for the sake of the city, with agility and immediacy.

August 25, 2017 will forever be a day of infamy in Houston, Texas. That was the day the historic and catastrophic Hurricane Harvey hit our city, and lingered for days, causing unprecedented destruction. Because we are a Church of House Churches, we had the power of one church and we were able to mobilize thousands immediately through our distributed channels of House Church leadership. We had literally every House Church working in their areas of the city within hours of the end of the hurricane. It was a terrible event for our city, but I will always remember those days with some pride because of the way our church responded as one church to care for our city.

In February 2021, a historic freeze hit our city. That week almost the entire state of Texas lost power. The water pipes in our Houston homes, built an hour from the Gulf of Mexico, were not built to endure the sustained record low temperatures. People all throughout our city were without water and electricity. Then when the water lines thawed, water rushed into homes destroying many properties. People had to turn off the water to their house, plumbers were unavailable or gouging prices, and because of cracked water pipes, days passed where people couldn't turn on their water to drink, bathe, or cook. Because we are a Church of

House Church we were able to immediately disburse into the homes of people across our city. Within hours, hundreds of people were trained across many dozens of House Churches on how to do simple pipe repairs, where otherwise they were told they would be waiting weeks without water in their homes, for their families.

Agility, accountability, and elevated collective impact are the beautiful benefits of being one church made up of many House Churches. Isolation, fragility, and impotence are potential consequences of being individual and isolated House Churches.

A church can be distributed and decentralized, and still have some centralization for accountability, encouragement, direction, and mission. Titus had some centralized leadership over the decentralized House Churches.

CHAPTER 3

DISTRIBUTED LEADERSHIP

I am grateful when I get some low-hanging fruit on otherwise complex topics. Distributed church leadership is one of those complex topics with some low hanging biblical fruit. In the Bible's letter to Titus, the apostle Paul tells Titus the reasons he sent him to take over the church he had planted. These are some verses I'm going to press into to clarify some important topics.

1, 2 Timothy, and Titus are often referred to as the pastoral letters. These are good gifts given to us by God for pastors as we seek to lead His people in His church. The Timothy letters have much to say about the heart and mind of Paul, and offer some perspective on pastoral leadership in the church.

The letter to Titus contains some of these pastoral and leadership elements as well. But Titus gives us even more insight into the purposes and structure of a church.

Paul tells Titus in chapter one and the beginning of chapter two, "the reason I left you in Crete was to straighten out what was unfinished…appoint leaders in every town as I directed you" (Titus 1:5), and "teach what is in accord with sound doctrine" (Titus 2:1).

These three directives are guides for me, and for those I lead, giving clarity for our purpose as leaders. We exist as pastors to straighten out what is unfinished, to appoint pastors for every person in our church, and teach sound doctrine.

We are to "straighten out what was unfinished." Paul planted a church in Crete, and there were things that still needed to be worked out. That's comforting. I'm grateful to know that the epic church planter Paul didn't get it all right super quick. And he needed help to move it forward.

It seems that Paul brought in Titus because Paul was compelled to carry on his calling as an evangelist in other places. And Paul was also brilliant at empowering other leaders to multiply the work beyond himself.

Paul wanted Titus to straighten out some things. Based on what Paul practiced elsewhere, this straightening out had to do with creating and correcting ministries to meet needs in the church and in the community. And, developing and deploying leaders to make disciples and pastor people in their city.

We are also to "teach what is in accord with sound doctrine." Pastors/elders/overseers are to protect and provide sound doctrine for God's people. We are to teach people sound doctrine, and teach them how to teach themselves. We are called to entrust biblical truths to reliable people who will also teach others.

And, we are to "appoint elders in every town as I directed you." Somehow, through Paul's ministry, the gospel had spread quickly around Crete. There were believers in villages and communities and towns throughout Crete. Paul would preach the gospel, and people would believe in Jesus and receive Him.

When Paul sent one of his proteges Titus to Crete, he had some clarity on what Titus was immediately supposed to do, and not do. Paul was clear that he did not want Titus building a ministry around himself. Paul didn't want Titus to go to all of the cities and be their pastor, or have all of the people in the cities come to him as their primary pastor. Paul didn't want the spreading of the gospel and the making of disciples to be limited to how fast Titus could travel to meet with people. If Titus was going to build on the evangelistic work of Paul, and if disciples were going to be made all around Crete, there had to be a distributed and decentralized way to accomplish this task that involved more than centering around one person. The discipleship movement would have been hindered had it hinged on one person.

Paul didn't want Titus to go to every town. And Paul didn't want the believers in every town to get to Titus. Paul didn't want Titus to disciple every believer. Paul wanted everyone to have access to an elder/overseer/pastor. Titus then, was called to appoint elders and to lead these elders. And, the elders/pastors would lead the people.

This was not about Titus creating a central place for the believers in Crete to come to. And, this was not about Titus being the central person who was the primary pastor for every person. This was about decentralizing discipleship away from the place where Titus was. And, this was about distributing pastoral leadership to others, not only Titus.

Decentralization and distribution of pastoral leadership are crucial components of the early church disciple-making movements.

Practically, movements can't be limited to a person. There's no one strong enough, enduring enough, wise enough, omnipresent enough, to carry a movement. Jesus is powerful and omnipresent and all wise, but He is the obvious and first example of distributing leadership to start a movement.

The priesthood of the believer is a new element for the New Testament church. In the Old Testament, under the old covenants, priests were the ones empowered and entrusted with the duties of the sacraments, teaching, and oversight of the people.

In the New Testament, under the new covenant of Christ, with the giving of His Spirit to every believer, the priesthood of the believer is a new identity that requires its presence and practice within the church if gospel movements are to occur.

The priesthood of the believer is the powerful presence of God within each of His followers to empower them to do the work of God, on God's behalf. Rather than a selected, separated, and elevated clergy present in the old covenant, the new covenant has appointed every believer to be a priest on behalf of God.

We are required to adjust away from old covenant practices of priesthood. Jesus is the High Priest, and He has appointed His followers to be priests on His behalf. Identified as "the priesthood of believers" (I Peter 2:9), Jesus has empowered every one of His followers with the Holy Spirit, and has assigned gifts which these believers will practice in order to be a part of Jesus's work in and through the church.

An adjustment of this understanding of the priesthood requires an adjustment of the practice of clergy. Centuries one through three, rapid gospel movements were happening, and the decentralization and distribution of pastoral leadership was elevating. Since the 4th century, the church has centralized place and priest, and elevated and separated pastors from the people. Many have essentially translated the old covenant Levites and turned them into New Testament clergy. The ones who are educated in the right places, with the right degree or pedigree, are the new priests. They are centered in a certain place, and have certain duties that only those with the proper credentials can perform. Just like the Old Testament priests.

Paul was leading the church to move away from central priest, and central place. Paul was helping Titus to see this new adjustment away from temple priests, to the priesthood of every believer. All believers have priestly duties, and some are called to pastor.

People still have specific calling. Paul had a special calling. So did Timothy and Titus and many others. So do many today. But, the calling of these people was to equip and empower people to pastor and lead and make disciples, not to take these roles away from the people.

Paul wanted Titus to go among the people and appoint pastors. Paul wanted all of the people in all of the places to have a pastor. He wanted everyone to have access to a pastor. And those pastors came from among the people, not an elevated, separated, spiritual position like a priest.

Of course, the people would have wanted Paul to be their personal pastor. And if they couldn't get Paul, then at least give them the next best appointment, in this case Titus. But, Paul told Titus to appoint them a no name, not yet developed, from among them, pastor to oversee the people.

As an aside to address some regular questions on this topic: the full point of distributed leadership wasn't Paul opposing someone being financially supported by the church. He himself was, when the church could, or when it wasn't detrimental to that specific church, so that he could devote all of his time to the ministry God called him to. Paul made room Scripturally in several places for the church to financially support those leaders who devote all of their available time to the work of overseeing and discipleship.

But, such an elastic clause has been stretched out of context to mean that the work of a pastor is reserved for the vocation of a pastor. And, the requirements for the office of a vocational pastor have been distorted to such a degree that the opportunity has been removed for the ordinary believer in the body to become a pastor. A "normal" person can't pastor, only "clergy" can, is the functional understanding of a pastor. And, to become clergy, here are the requirements and expectations…

On the contrary, Jesus deployed really normal disciples with the mission of spreading the gospel and making disciples, which resulted in the beginnings of churches being planted around the world. Paul also raised up normal, not elevated or separated or super qualified leaders, who became pastors really quickly for churches he planted.

Scripture is clear that these men Jesus appointed weren't regarded as ready, or worthy. In fact, the priests and clergy rulers of the people saw them as "ordinary" men. The religious ruling parties in Israel discounted Jesus' disciples because they were ordinary. Of course, they didn't even think Jesus Himself had the credentials to teach the people.

Paul would share the gospel, people would be saved, he would choose leaders, prepare them with whatever time he had, then leave. He left, but didn't leave them alone.

Sometimes Paul would only be in town for a night. The longest time Paul would stay in one place was Ephesus- he was there for three and half years. He was in Antioch with Barnabas for a year teaching. But most of the time, Paul was in a place for days, or weeks, or at most months. Regardless of his time in a place, every time Paul was about identifying, preparing, appointing, and entrusting leaders.

Paul would continue to lead the leaders that he had entrusted to oversee the church. He would continue to lead them in person, by proxy, or by pen.

Paul would personally travel back to the churches he planted whenever he could. He longed to get back to the people who he had introduced to Jesus, to see how the church was doing, and to pour strength into the church. In person was his preference. But, he was only one person, and could only be in one place, at one time.

When Paul couldn't go in person, he often sent a proxy. He would send someone on his behalf to share a message with the church, to check on the wellbeing of the church, and to report back on their findings. Paul would prepare people to lead like he led, believe like he believed, and see what he saw. Paul was relieved when someone would come back to him and share a good report of a healthy church.

Paul would also often continue to lead by pen. Hence, our inspired Scriptures available to us today to give us insight into the workings of God within His church. Paul would send letters of encouragement, instruction, admonition, warnings, and rebuke. Paul wrote specifically for his audience in that community, while knowing his writings would be shared with many other churches, for many years to come.

When Paul appointed leadership, that leadership was not left alone to lead themselves. Paul ensured every leader continued to have a leader to guide them in doctrine and pastoring, to hold them accountable, and to step in where there were issues.

Titus was charged with the task of appointing leaders within the church. And, Paul gave Titus a list of qualifications for these pastors that would assist Titus as he fulfilled the task of selecting leaders. So, Jesus appointed Paul. Paul appointed Titus. Titus appointed elders.

Titus appointed pastors at the local level. So every person had a pastor, and every pastor had a pastor. Titus was pastored by Paul, Titus pastored the pastors in every city, and every person in every church in every city had a local pastor accessible to them. In this we see evidences of ongoing oversight and connectivity. Across the entire region of Crete, Titus was overseeing all of the elders and pastors of House Churches.

After a Sunday gathering, I was introduced to a couple who had just returned months before from living in a foreign country for a decade. They were working toward a church plant there in a location that was resistant to the gospel. The circumstances that led them to return to the States were difficult.

They were lonely and sad and tried to join several church communities, longing for some believers to live life together with as they healed, and discerned God's will for what was next in their lives. After being in another country church planting for so long, they couldn't stomach the western approach of attractional church models. These churches are commonly characterized by a weak or non-existent teaching of Scripture replaced with spiritual talks, in conjunction with shallow expressions of homogenized community. Such shallow expressions of community were now unusual and insufficient to them.

Through their experiences on the mission field and study of Scripture, history and the global church, their missiology and their ecclesiology had refined. And though they had given their lives to the making of disciples and the planting of the gospel through the planting of local churches, they were finding great difficulty planting their lives in any church here.

Somehow they discovered us. After gathering together with us for around a month, they asked someone if they could help broker a conversation between us. As someone introduced us and briefly explained their story,

I braced myself for the possibility of whatever direction the conversation may flow. In creating a disruptive environment, especially more-so than in my previous traditionally and culturally acceptable contexts, opposing opinions are expressed vigorously by people sensing a need to defend their norms which are being opposed.

So, when they told me that though they had gathered into our community together for a month, and they still didn't know who the leader of this thing was, I began internally preparing my response. They had been telling their friends locally and internationally about this new church community they had found. Their friends asked them who the lead pastor was. They said that they didn't know, and their friends couldn't believe it. It seemed incredulous, unusual, and reckless to them. They didn't see a name on a church bulletin, on a billboard or church sign. My name wasn't even on our website.

As I was about to begin to biblically explain our ecclesiological approach, they said, "We love it. We've looked for it around our city, and haven't been able to find it. We are so thankful for what you are working towards here."

I said, "Ummmm ... thanks!?" I was relieved and encouraged. I continued "We actually do get these kinds of thoughts shared with us often. And, it's uncanny how many former foreign missionaries gather into community in our church, for the same reasons."

CHAPTER 4

HOUSE CHURCH

MACRO/MICRO HYBRID. HOUSE CHURCH & CORPORATE GATHERINGS.

There is a massive bifurcation in the church along the lines of macro and micro. Much of the western church approach for many decades has been built around large, fully centralized expressions of church. Recently, the retaliation to mega decentralization has generally been an equal and opposite fully decentralized and disconnected micro church approach.

And much of the conversation around mega and micro church really has nothing to do with structure or approach, or even theology. It mainly has to do with size. Churches that share the exact same structure, approach, and theology, but differ in sizes, often seem to have a sense of more effectiveness or correctness over another. Small churches sometimes think they are the proper approach rather than the "shallow or personality driven mega church model". Large churches sometimes think they are more effective than small churches, due to more people in attendance. In the end though, they are both super centralized church structures, one just performed better than the other.

Different streams, denominations, networks, and affiliations, usually have the same type of church happening, just with different degrees of effectiveness and size. Therefore, attendance and style often becomes the differentiating factor in conversations around correctness.

Most churches really aren't that different from one another. There are of course nuanced differences in theology, but many churches in comparable conversations are preaching the gospel of Christ, and teaching the Scriptures. And there are differences stylistically, as churches have contemporary or traditional approaches. But this is cosmetic. Though nuanced differences in theology and styles, the structure and leadership is almost identical.

And the consistency is…heavy centralization in people and place, leadership and space.

One alternative to the same contemporary approach, is acknowledging the existence of the earliest expression of church we find in Scripture: House Church.

It's impossible to read Scripture and not see House Church.

It's a weird phrase to some people. Some think it's possible in some places culturally, but not necessary contemporarily or globally. Others think it was good then, or maybe there, but not necessary now and here.

To others, it's sacrosanct. It's the way. It's the only way. There's no need or reason for anything other than. To some, the words House Church connote a picture of disconnected, disenfranchised, distant, or doctrinally arrogant people.

To those who believe in House Church, the opposition often means that people are shallow, content to sometimes sit in a seat and sing some songs and listen to some sermons, but not commit to real community. You're for it, or you're not. There seems to be no in between. No both/and. No hybrid.

Whatever your opinion, the biblical existence of House Church has to be acknowledged. And, something has to be reconciled. Either it was good then, but not needed now. Or, it began this way for a reason, and should continue to be practiced in the church today.

The common Biblical phrase, "To the church that meets in so-and-so's house," is obviously a House Church. We see them throughout the Scriptures.

"Give my greetings to the brothers and sisters at Laodicea, and to Nympha and the church in her house." Colossians 4:15

"Greet Priscilla & Aquila, my co-workers in Christ Jesus ... Greet also the church that meets at their house." Romans16:3-5

" ... to Apphia our sister and Archippus our fellow soldier—and to the church that meets in your home." Philemon 1:2

Everyone who reads Scripture can accept this reality. There was a church that met in someone's house. There is universal agreement (with the exception of those who love to create an argument out of empty space) that House Church existed, at some point, at least in the places listed in these verses and others.

The argument arises when we wonder if the house was just a humble beginning, a necessary place and function until they could get a real building, a real place, to become a real or healthy or self-sustaining church? Was the end goal a church in a house? Or was that temporary until they could get enough money raised, enough people, and finally get a bigger place?

Or, was House Church a construct intended to keep every church small? Should church sizes be constrained by the square footage capacity of a house? If the size of a church is intended to be constrained by its container of a house, then what happens to people who come to the house, when there is no room in the house? Do they gather somewhere else in a bigger container? Is the house used for another function of the church?

I'll spoil some of this talk later. But for now, let's talk about what House Church is. We can give some clarity by comparison.

HOUSE CHURCH vs. SMALL GROUP

What's the difference between a Small Group, and a House Church?

What's the difference between a leader or teacher, and a House Church pastor?

It might first be helpful to discuss the qualities of what makes a church, a church. Some people quote "where two or three are gathered" Jesus is there with us, as the definition of a church. But, Jesus is also with us as individuals. We as individual believers have the presence of and are the temple of the Holy Spirit. But, I am not a church.

The local church matters to the presence and spread of the gospel in a place. Paul would share the gospel, and immediately start a church. The church would endure beyond the individual. The church would be the core of the gospel work of making disciples in a city.

One way I define the church is "the body of Christ gathered locally, all around the world."

Beyond the Spirit of God working in and through the lives of individuals who follow Jesus, God created the church, the locally gathered community of Christ followers. The church has intentionality, value, purpose, and identity. In these many values and purposes, the church also has certain characteristics that define its existence:

A church has leadership. - Paul appointed leaders.

A church has authority. - obey your leaders and submit to their authority.

A church has mission. - to each one the manifestation of the Spirit has been given for the common good.

A church has diversity. - no Gentile or Jew, circumcised or uncircumcised, barbarian, Scythian, slave or free, but Christ is all.

A church has connectivity. - body, each one of you is a part of it.

A church has local identity. - to the church in Rome, Corinth, Philippi, etc.

A House Church is a church. A House Church has these characteristics that are present in a church, but not present in individuals, or even in most groups.

A church has a pastor who is accountable to God for its leadership. A church has diversity, not homogeneity. A church is connected eternally and presently, and is more than friends, it's a family. A church has a complete mission for the spread of the gospel and the common good.

A group or class generally has a couple of purposes it is expected to accomplish. Teaching, some community, occasional benevolence, but a group has intended limitations.

On the other hand, a House Church carries the full mission of a church (vs. a para-church organization, or a class, or a group).

A House Church has an identified, equipped, empowered, pastor, not only a leader or teacher. A House Church pastor is the front line for all discipleship, community, and meeting of needs for an entire small body of believers. (Also, a House Church pastor baptizes, does weddings and funerals, and can lead communion at their discretion.)

A House Church is responsible to ensure every person is equipped to and engaged in being discipled, and discipling someone else.

A House Church is responsible to ensure every person is engaged in a ministry, in serving in their city or world.

A House Church has diversity generationally, socio-economically, different ethnicities, different marital status, different places in their spiritual maturity, different spiritual gifting and ministries.

A House Church has community that is a diverse family more than homogenous friends.

A House Church carries an expectation of evangelism, equipping and expecting every person engaged in the growth and multiplication of the House Church by bringing new people into the church community.

A House Church is responsible for its own benevolence, caring for all of the needs of one another first within that House Church community.

(Diversity is such a huge part of the biblical, historical, and global church. So, I've separated and expanded this discussion into its own chapter later.)

We've briefly looked at characteristics that exist within a church, but what makes a House Church a church, and not a small group?

House Churches are small. Small Groups are small. So, we're the same, right? As we read above, a leader is not the same thing as a pastor, a group is not the same thing as a church.

Small Groups and Sunday School classes have important roles. God has used these to accomplish some great things, even in my own life. However, the overwhelming majority of people in these groups do not see them as their church. So there is a limit to what these groups do. Since they are not identified as a church, or expected to be, the rest of the stuff, the bigger stuff, is left to "the church". Sunday school and small groups are limited in their expectations, and consequently in their impact, to function fully as a church.

If these are the elements that make a church a church, these are also the elements that make a House Church a church, not a group.

Before a Church of House Churches:

In the church I grew up in I never saw benevolence occurring in the church. I'm sure it happened in our church. I just wasn't personally participating in that within my community. So I didn't get the privilege to step in and meet others people's needs.

In fact, I really didn't hear about other people's needs. There wasn't a context where we could really openly share struggles. People would sometimes share prayer requests, usually for the needs of others. Sometimes, people would even say that they had an "unspoken" prayer request, like they had a need, but didn't want to say what it was. Meeting needs is predicated on a culture and a context where needs are shared openly with one another, so that needs can be prayed for, and needs can be met within that context.

I also didn't live in community with people of different generations. I knew who some older people were. And I sat in auditoriums with people of different ages. And when I was younger, older people taught me the Bible in a class, and did a phenomenal job. But, the church I grew up in, and the churches I led and served, generally didn't live in close discipleship community with people of different generations.

I didn't serve in ministries to meet needs in our city. There were occasional big serving days to do something in our city. And sometimes we would have a work day at the church building. And when I got older I went on some week long mission trips. But, beyond that day or two a year, and that special week, I was never never giving my time, passions, and gifts to a ministry that was meeting real needs in our city, and sharing the gospel with the people they served.

I had the gift of a close relationship with an associate pastor in our church who discipled me. But, most people didn't. They couldn't. He was only one guy, and there were only a few other associate pastors, for the hundreds of people in our church. Most people didn't have access to a pastor, unless some major issue was happening in their life, or they made an appointment for counseling.

I never discipled anyone. I just didn't know how to do that. I rarely thought about the need for it, or any personal responsibility to do that. It wasn't talked about much or at all in the churches I grew up in and led. I never heard of discipling someone else. If I wanted to disciple someone, I had no idea what that would look like, how I would begin, or what I would do or say. I had the Bible poured into me for years. I knew a lot of biblical truth, and I loved and followed Jesus. But I never personally poured this vast amount of input back into anyone, until I became a pastor. And, even then for many years as a pastor, I never personally discipled anyone, just generally pastored the masses.

I had good classes that taught me the Bible. And I was around some really good people who led those classes and programs. As good as these church models are, none compare to what is experienced when one gets involved with a House Church. In a House Church, people get a front row seat to participate in the big stuff God is doing in people's lives, and they get to be a part of that story forever.

CHAPTER 5

HOUSE CHURCH AND PASTOR OR SMALL GROUP AND LEADER

W e'll assume that everyone reading this by now accepts that House Churches existed in Scripture. But for many, the contemporary translation of House Church is…small groups.

While accepting that House Church existed, many would say that their smaller church expression presently performs the functions of House Church, just calling it something different, and maybe or maybe not meeting in a home. House Churches were small, small groups are small. Therefore, they're the same.

The typical conversation on the topic goes something like this: "Yeah, we have House Churches. We just call them small groups. The early church had large gatherings, then smaller groups for community. We also have large corporate gatherings, and we have smaller communities. We just call ours small groups. Or Sunday School. But we are essentially doing the same thing."

Right!? Or…were House Churches different from small groups? Or Sunday School classes?

They were.

Small groups and Sunday School aren't bad. No way! So many good things have come from small groups and from Sunday School!

But, they don't accomplish the fullness of what House Church was, or was intended to be. Small Groups and Sunday School, by nature and intention, form and function, are not designed to be what House Church was designed to be.

The difference is dependent primarily upon two things:

- Elevating class or group..............to church.
- Elevating leader or teacher..........to pastor.

A small group leader (or Sunday School teacher) has an important role. God uses people in these roles in phenomenal ways. But, the overwhelming majority of people in these leadership positions are not seen as the pastor of this group of people. There is a limit to what these small group leaders and teachers are expected to do. They are not identified as the pastor, or expected to be. The rest of the stuff, the bigger churchy stuff, is left to the clergy, the staff, and the "real" pastors.

Pastors would all say that pastoring is much more than teaching. Pastoring is cultivating a community that comprehensively reflects the full biblical descriptions of community, not just aspects of a church, but a complete and healthy church. Pastoring is taking oversight and responsibility of the comprehensive condition of people in a spiritual community. Pastoring is directing a community toward their mission of spreading the gospel and making disciples. Pastoring is making sure that every person under their care is engaging in accountable, and discipleship oriented relationships. Pastoring is leading people to grow in the grace of giving. Pastoring is leading people to meet one another's needs. Pastoring is walking with people through significant trials. Pastoring is accountability and church discipline. Pastoring is raising up leaders. Pastoring is…a lot.

House Church Pastors fully pastor their House Church. They oversee discipleship relationships for every person under their care. They are the front-line for initial counseling and benevolence, they do weddings and funerals, baptisms and communion, and the community they cultivate is completely dependent upon their leadership. They baptize people in pools, or in the corporate gatherings, because they have been the ones to lead and pastor their people.

They are decentralized and entrusted. They are identified as the pastor to their people. There is no one else to pastor the people in their House Church if their House Church pastor does not. This is their little church, their House Church, to fully pastor. They are accountable for these people.

Some ask why we call a House Church pastor, a pastor. I say, why would we not!? Do we not expect them to pastor? Why would we call a pastor a leader, and not a pastor? Do we not want Small Group leaders to fully pastor and shepherd their people? Or are we limiting the expectation of how much we want Small Group leaders or Sunday School teachers to pastor the lives of their people? And to fill the pastoral gap, we have created an elevated and separated clergy to do the full pastoral things.

If we're not limiting their expectation of pastoring, let's call them a pastor! Let's identify them. Let's equip them. Let's empower them. Let's have their church community that they pastor know that this person is their pastor. Let's not give anyone in the church anywhere else to go to circumvent their House Church pastor to get to the "real" pastor/staff/clergy. Let's remove ourselves as the more powerful pastors, and put the House Church Pastor in the primary place of pastor for their people.

One week after a simple Sunday gathering, a recent college graduate approached me. He had just moved to our town, and this was the first time he had stepped into anything attached to our church. I asked him how he found us, as I always ask, since we don't do any marketing. He said he heard about us from someone he worked with, so he did some initial investigation, was intrigued because he had never been a part of a church like this, and wanted to take some next steps of discovery.

He asked me where the Young Adult group met. I told him we don't have a Young Adult group. He was surprised, and said, "You don't have young adults!?" I told him that in fact, we did have hundreds of young adults his age in our church community. But, that they weren't a group. They were spread throughout our many different House Churches. And they all had House Church pastors. He was surprised, reluctant, but willing to give House Church a try.

A few weeks later I ran into him again in the mix of our Sunday Gathering. I asked him if he had taken the steps to get into a House Church. He then started telling me about the coffee he had with his House Church pastor, and an older man in his House Church who was going to be meeting with him, and about the ministry he had gotten connected to. I interrupted him, and said, "Wait. Did you just say 'My House Church pastor?' Have you ever said that before?" He started telling me how reluctant he was to try this, it was so different than he's ever experienced in church, but how this has been such a phenomenal entry into church and a new city.

Fast forward some months. He happens to meet many other young adults through serving, or random Sunday Gathering connection, or an occasional Young Adult event. Then, as also often happens, he met a girl, dated her, and married her. And, his House Church pastor, who happens to be a captain in the Fire Department, did their pre-marital counseling, and their destination wedding. (By the way, I would have loved to have been invited to perform their wedding, especially at that destination, but I wasn't invited to do so. Their pastor, their House Church pastor, was who they knew best.)

Based upon these initial simple definitions of pastor and church, there's a pretty clear difference between what makes a

House Church a church, and a House Church pastor a pastor. And, what keeps a group a group, and a leader a leader.

SIZE OF A HOUSE CHURCH:

These descriptions of duties highlight some of the reasons why we want House Churches to remain a manageable size. Pastoring is complex and comprehensive. If a House Church is too big, a House Church pastor will feel exasperated and inadequate. Their life will get out of healthy balance. House Church pastors have full-time jobs in the marketplace. They have a limited amount of time, and because of this, we limit the amount of people they will pastor. We want a House Church pastor to have a healthy life in every way- with their spouse and kids, physically, relationally, emotionally, spiritually...too many people to pastor will create an unhealthy situation.

If a House Church is too big, people will not be pastored well. In a large crowd, people can be overlooked by the pastor and get lost in the community. And, if people don't feel loved and seen and can't be pastorally developed in a House Church, where will this happen? They'll be hurt, feel invisible, under-discipled, and possibly leave the church wounded.

People often ask how big should a House Church ideally be? 12 like Jesus led? After all, we're not better than Jesus!? 40, that's a pretty biblical number - 40 years wandering in the wilderness, 40 days fasting in the desert...But, 7 - that's the number of perfection. And, 3! 3 is the idea of the Trinity, 3 days from death to resurrection, 3 days in the whale.

So, what's the perfect number?!?!? I say...medium. When people ask what size is best, I say medium. Too small feels pretty awkward, and is hard to get significant stuff accomplished. Too big, people get lost, and the pastor gets overwhelmed. But medium, medium feels pretty good.

When it's too small, we can press in and uncover the reasons for the lack of growth. Are people who are engaged in this House Church not pursuing conversations and relationships in the community, and praying for and inviting their unchurched and unsaved friends? Are people coming to the House Church but not returning, because the community is not welcoming them, or the House Church pastor doesn't respond to them? Why is this House Church staying small for a significant season?

If it's too big, are we not developing other people to entrust pastoral leadership to? Is the House Church pastor being over-protective of what he leads, rather than thinking that healthy multiplication moves the mission of the gospel within a city? Are there no presently visibly viable people to potentially pastor, and if so, how do we find and disciple and develop them?

Also, sometimes people question whether or not House Churches are "open or closed." Meaning, do we close the group down to new people so that we can just build closeness within this specific group of people? Or, is the House Church continually open to new people coming in whenever they decide.

I have a hard time imagining a person walking into a House Church in the first century, looking for community, disciple-ship, or considering Christianity, and being told that there is not room for them. Can you hear James in Jerusalem saying, "sorry, this group is closed, thanks for making an attempt to seek after Christ by joining into a diverse discipleship community, but we're focusing on intimacy here." It seems unusual, unlikely, and counterintuitive to the mission.

This highlights a reason why we don't have a hardline number of acceptable attenders. To keep everything in balance, House Churches are always open and available and interested in receiving anyone looking for a diverse discipleship community. This keeps at the forefront of ongoing mission the super impor-tance of continually developing the next pastor who will take a portion of these people and strategically plant another House Church when the time, size, and health is right and ready.

Early on in the life of our church as we were continuing to form, I was also having to personally learn this approach of distributed pastoral leadership. I was used to decades of being the point for all pastoral needs, and I had never been in this environment myself, much less created and cultivated this kind of context.

One day I happened to hear about a child who had a significant medical event. They were rushed to the Emergency Room. So, I left my family, and rushed to the hospital. I got to the ER desk and told the attendant that I was there to see this specific person. She asked me if I was immediate family, I told her that I was their pastor (pastors in our area are treated by hospitals, and other places, with the same access as immediate family). She looked at me suspiciously and told me that a person who identified himself as their pastor was already back with the family.

I was taken aback for a moment. Who could this be? And, why wasn't it me? I soon realized that the person pastoring the family was in fact their House Church pastor. He heard about this need before I did because he lived in close connectivity with this family. And, he was the person who should have been the point to be pastoring and praying with and comforting and encouraging these parents, because he was their personal pastor.

After I realized who this person was claiming to be their pastor, I also remembered that this was in fact the plan. Not just the plan for Church Project, but this was God's plan for His church. It was a better plan. It was more scalable, more personal, more durable, more effective. This was less dependent upon one person or centralized office, it is more distributed and sustainable.

As well, immediately, an entire House Church was activated. They stepped in like a small church to take care of the other kids in the family, to bring meals for weeks, to visit the family in the hospital, to pray for them, and to give toward their massive unexpected medical and out of pocket expenses.

I do at times step in and pastor people in these types of situations. I love our people too. And, some things are so significant, that other layers of support and pastoring are helpful. But, it's not all dependent upon the people paid to pastor.

Furthermore, I'm not robbing people in our body who have the calling and gifting and desire to pastor. People feel alive when they are living out their calling. Our job is to equip them to do this. My role is to create a context and cultivate leaders to do the work God has called them to do. My job was to then to encourage that House Church pastor for the phenomenal job he and the House Church did loving and caring for those in need in this situation.

I realized, I remembered, I celebrated. Then I went home to be with my family.

CHAPTER 6

DEVELOPING A HOUSE CHURCH PASTOR

Discovering and developing new House Church pastors is the way our impact increases and ministry continues beyond the elders, and the staff pastors. If a House Church is healthy, most likely it will grow (there are always mitigating circumstances of slow growth in a healthy context). If a House Church grows and has only one House Church pastor to accommodate their growth, the House Church will not be adequately cared for, and will eventually become unhealthy. Growth without multiplication leads to atrophy.

Preparing the next House Church pastor is crucial for health and growth. And, multiplication of House Churches and House Church pastors follows in the model of Jesus with His disciples, Paul with the first missionaries, and the early church with its House Church movements across a city.

A high responsibility of church leadership is choosing and approving other leaders for the church. Overseers must take seriously the calling to shepherd their people, even when that shepherding is happening through others who have been appointed. Whoever has been chosen as a House Church pastor has been entrusted to represent Christ to His local body, and to replicate the heart and lifestyle and responsibilities of an approved and committed shepherd.

Because of this responsibility, every pastor has to be tested and proven. It takes at minimum several months for us to discover and develop a new House Church pastor—though, in most cases more time is desired in order to know and develop them well. Apprenticing is a great way to facilitate this training. When Paul trained Timothy, he said, "You know me. You know all about my life, my teachings, my doctrine, my way of life. You know all about me" (2 Tim. 3:10). In the same way, people should know the pastor's life and be able to follow their example.

We have a saying: "House Churches beget House Churches, and pastors beget pastors." Paul, in a sense, begat Timothy. It wasn't a formal class training—it was life on life.

We can never entrust a ministry to someone we don't know well. Even being a member on church roll isn't qualification (though we personally don't have membership in this sense). We must confidently know their level of commitment and consistency before we entrust others to their care. We must know their interaction with others, their gifts, integrity, and their leadership. We must know their condition spiritually, theologically, and philosophically. Everyone has to get the DNA of the broader church before they begin leading.

The goal is to transfer DNA and values to everyone—from the original leaders on down. Pastoral training in the context of our local church is the best way to infuse everyone with the same DNA. We vet pastors for a long time, and every House Church pastor comes from within an existing House Church. We've known them, seen their lives, proven their leadership, gotten to know their doctrine, and listened to them teach. Even if someone has come from another church and another position of leadership, we need to know that they know us and believe in what we are doing.

After the pastor has been identified by his House Church, trained by the existing pastors, and been a part of our mission for a sufficient amount of time, we have an incubator. This is a small cohort of pastors and their spouses who will spend a month together, drilling more deeply into the expectations and responsibilities of their roles.

Then, the elders have final approval before appointing someone to the role of a House Church pastor. Finally, once we have dug into acute ideas of doctrine with them, they are proven and ready. They then need a healthy core to start with them, a healthy host with the gifts of hospitality, and multiplying out of an existing House Church in a healthy way.

A brief word about hospitality. I define hospitality as: "you want people to be in your home, and people want to be in your home". If you don't want people in your home, you probably don't have the gift of hospitality. And, if people don't really look forward to being in your home, you may not have the gift of hospitality. *I.e. If your house is dark or dirty, or you have leg-licking dogs, people won't want to come back.* Disclaimer: even people with the gift of hospitality don't always want people in their home. Some weeks will be hard to gear up for it, but even then, at the end of the night, those people are usually glad they did.

When we are considering multiplying a House Church, we don't want to hurt one House Church to help another. So we want the House Church remaining to be a healthy size, with sufficient leadership, and happy about this plant. I describe the planting of another House Church as the emotional equivalent of sending a kid off to college. We have prepared them for this moment, it's time, and if they stay too long, it will get weird and unhealthy.

Every pastor needs a pastor. Each House Church pastor has a pastor assigned to them who meets with them, checks on them, cares for them, and is aware of all arenas of their life. We have conversations about the health of their personal life, the health and practices of their House Church, and their development of others for multiplication.

We also have ongoing training with our House Church pastors. Every other month we have a corporate meeting with all House Church pastors. Our staff pastors who oversee House Church send out videos and reminders throughout the month.

Preparing and launching a pastor will take time, but the pastors will still need to grow and mature, so the training never ends.

And, each House Church pastor has constant access to a staff pastor who is experienced and trained in sensitive and difficult situations. When abuse or tragedy happens, and the businessperson who is a House Church pastor needs support, they always have it immediately available. The staff serves House Church.

With all of these preparations and processes, it should be stated that we must be comfortable appointing pastors who are not fully ready—just like the disciples weren't. But we should make sure they're ready enough. Jesus could have spent many more years with His disciples before He commissioned them, and they still would not have been all the way ready. Jesus got them ready enough, and then continued to work with them so that they grew and matured once they had been sent. The preparation, plus the presence of the Spirit in their lives, will be enough.

The strength of a church rises and falls on the strength of its community, and the strength of our community rises and falls on our House Church pastors. Our pastors are people I love, respect, and enjoy. I like them. I want to spend more time with them than I get to. I depend on them. They give their lives for the gospel and the church, and we would not exist or be healthy without them.

Discovering and developing House Church pastors is enriching to the life of the smaller group of staff pastors and elders of the larger body of Christ. Having colleagues—people in the trenches with you—is essential to the overall health of a church's leadership. My pastoral colleagues are doctors, fire-fighters, attorneys, police officers, oil and gas executives—this makes life rich, diverse, and fun. And, these highly capable people feel a great sense of trust and responsibility when given a House Church to pastor.

A man who was a high level executive at one of the world's largest corporations moved to our area and started visiting our church. He said he loved everything we were about, and wanted to start leading here with us. He told me about the great church he was a part of before (it is a great church by many measures), his leadership in that place, and how he wanted to do that here. He wanted to become a House Church pastor.

I told him that I was very encouraged by his heart to serve and use his gifts in the local church, and that he wanted to do that here. And, I could sense he had a strong relationship with Jesus, and phenomenal leadership skills. But, I told him that he would need to graft his life into the life of our church first. We would need to see that he is faithfully engaged, watch how he submits to authority, how he serves with humility, and that he truly adopts our nuances and differences as a church for this community.

At first he was taken aback. He was a little surprised that what was a little church at the time, and a young pastor at the time, wouldn't immediately jump on an opportunity to leverage a leader like himself.

But, I wouldn't compromise the clear calling for our church just to leverage the leadership and giving and gifting of this person. We had to protect our calling.

I was surprised he stayed. But he did. And he's been with us for many years now, leading in many ways among us.

I'm always surprised by the level of intimidation when a high capacity leader in the marketplace becomes a House Church pastor. Someone who leads boards and many layers of leadership often gets nervous at the thought of pastoring people.

Actually, I get nervous when someone doesn't get nervous. Of course there should be some sense of confidence in the calling and equipping to execute the role of a pastor. But, if there's no sense of humility, there may be hubris present. Pastoring requires leadership, but it's much more than leadership. I'm grateful for humble pastors, who apply their gifting and calling to pastor their House Church.

CHAPTER 7

LARGE CORPORATE GATHERINGS

MACRO/MICRO HYBRID. HOUSE CHURCH & CORPORATE GATHERINGS.

While *it's impossible to read Scripture* and not see the presence and purpose of House Churches, it is also impossible to read Scripture and not see the presence and purpose of large corporate gatherings of believers.

It seems the majority of people who buy into the true House Church expression of church get far away from any connectivity to a large, centralized church, and/or any large corporate gatherings of believers. Perhaps they do this because there is no where else for them to go. Or perhaps it's because they can't see any hope of their centralized church changing. Or perhaps it's because they have been disillusioned with the corporate church as they have known it, and see no value or redemption in it.

So, an individual isolated House Church is the answer for them. They step into a small gathering of diverse people in a living room led by a pastor, carrying out the mission of the gospel in their city. It's new, it's intimate, and it's exciting.

But, God has also seemed to value the large corporate gathering of His people. There is a value to corporate worship. In the Old Testament, people gathered regularly for feasts and festivals and the worship was pretty phenomenal, planned out and prepared and had a ton of people present. In the New Testament, where House Churches were birthed, large corporate gatherings still happened. The apostles taught people by the thousands. They were kicked out of the Temple courts and rented Solomon's Colonnade, a lecture hall contiguous to the Temple, for weekly gatherings for thousands of people.

I'm not sure what smaller communities will look like in Heaven. I'm not sure what diversity will look like in Heaven with age, gender, skin color, etc. But, the glimpses God has given into corporate worship of His people in Heaven, joining with angels, will be phenomenal.

God seems to love the corporate gathering of His people in the Old Testament, the New Testament, and in Heaven.

About 7-8 years after I planted Church Project, I was extra tired. More tired than the usual tired. I needed rest more than I realized, and I thought maybe the problems were different and deeper. But thankfully, our elders could see that what I needed was rest. So, they encouraged me to take 4 weeks off one summer. Instead of resisting as I had before because of my fear of what would happen to the church if I wasn't around, I accepted. (Even with all of our distributed leadership and decentralized community, I still have my own struggles, that many/most pastors I know share, of fears of what could happen if I step away too long. Thankfully, God has grown me past this - mainly due to me taking appropriate time away to sabbath.)

Week one, it was good to be away. Week two was a little harder. After not being in a corporate worship gathering for a couple of weeks, I found myself really desiring to be in a gathering of believers who were singing songs to Jesus together, where the Word was being taught.

The next week, I went and sat in another church's Sunday gathering. It affected me emotionally. I missed the beauty of the body gathered. I loved the sound of hundreds of voices singing, and the sights of people with their Bibles opened. I didn't only miss my church, I missed the church.

During the pandemic, most churches didn't have in-person gatherings for a short while. It was the first time for many in their life that they weren't able to decide on their own whether or not to gather in person with other believers for worship. It was a good personal learning and corporate teaching opportunity to illuminate for us the reality that many believers around the world live with. Many believers globally have no opportunity to choose whether or not to gather with other believers corporately. Either there are too few believers to gather, or there is persecution preventing them from doing so.

And, some people would love to gather with other believers to experience what most have available to them weekly, but they don't have the health that enables them to get together. And some don't have resources of a car, a person, public transportation, or finances to help them travel to a regular corporate worship gathering. Not only is there so much good in a corporate gathering, it is a gift to have the choice to be able to be present.

The question becomes, how do we remain decentralized, and distribute leadership, while also having corporate gatherings? And if churches were forming in houses, where did large gatherings occur?

As we see House Churches happening, so we see corporate gatherings happening. Michael Kruger observes,

"*Thus, the church at a particular city seems to have been viewed as **a single unit–despite** the fact that it was probably **composed of multiple smaller congregations meeting in homes.** Some scholars even think that **all the house churches in these cities would have, on occasion, gathered together in a single meeting to worship** (1 Cor. 14.23) 72 or to hear Paul's letters being read (Rom. 16.3–16)." Michale Kruger*

The first church in Acts can't be overlooked. There was such beauty of the body distributed into House Church communities where discipleship, family, benevolence, and so many beautiful functions of the church took place.

But alongside of these House Churches, the believers also gathered regularly for corporate worship and teaching. Offerings were taken and laid at the apostle's feet to distribute as they best discerned. Songs were sung, Scriptures were taught, prayers were prayed.

The corporate gathering wasn't a replacement for House Church. The gatherings were accomplishing what wouldn't be accomplished in House Church. Teaching from the apostles was key for development of doctrine in the body. The beauty of the gathered body worshipping together was powerful. A room full of believers from across the city is good for the soul.

There are teachers who have been gifted to teach large groups, who are doctrinally developed, and the exercise of their gift for the corporate body is beneficial for the discipleship of the entire body. The apostles taught the church in Jerusalem. Barnabas went and found Paul and brought him to teach the church in Antioch for a year. Jesus taught many people many times on mountainsides.

Essentially, the Sunday Gathering supports House Church. The Sunday Gathering supports House Church by pastoring House Church leadership. In a Sunday Gathering, House Church pastors are developed alongside of their House Church body when they are being taught the Scriptures. House Church leadership is also growing in their pursuit of Jesus. They need to continue to be taught the Word and form their doctrine and biblical worldview. A pastor who is gifted to teach them does that every week, alongside of their own House Church.

House Church pastors also have an opportunity in the corporate gatherings to be led and poured into, rather than to lead. Every pastor is pouring into the lives of people regularly, while they themselves also need regular moments for someone to speak truth to them, to worship without the burden of leadership for a moment.

Maybe most importantly, having a common corporate gathering, where all House Churches gather for worship, helps protect the doctrine across all of the House Churches. If House Churches wrestle through the same passages of Scripture together, that have been preached on Sunday, there is intrinsic protection.

Where you have distributed leadership and decentralization, there must be a way to have common doctrine and direction, and accountability for this doctrine to be kept. Teaching Scripture in the weekly corporate gathering, and alignment across House Churches for continuation of conversation on that same passage of Scripture, is one of the greatest protections against doctrinal deviation.

When members of a House Church hear a sermon, and then they are wrestling and digging into and discussing together this passage of Scripture as a House Church community, the doctrine that has been shared corporately gives guidance and protection from deviation into doctrinal error.

The Sunday Gathering supports House Church by protecting doctrine, developing House Church pastors, and prompting tensions that need to be resolved in House Church community.

In the Scriptures, historically, and globally, we also see the practice of simplicity in the corporate gatherings. There was nothing attractive or attractional happening. Environments were not being created for entertainment, or even primarily evangelistic investigation. Consideration of a visiting unbeliever was taken into account with explanation of spiritual things. But, the gathering was for the believer to worship and hear the Scriptures taught to them. The draw into the church wasn't based on the wowness of the weekend corporate gathering.

There is actually a liturgy given to pastors concerning the gatherings of believers. We have distilled these to include: singing, silence, sermon, story, and Scripture reading. As was practiced, then prescribed to us by the apostles, a corporate gathering should include the teaching the Scriptures/sermon, singing spiritual songs and hymns, moments of silence and reflection, Scriptures read aloud, and sharing of stories/testimonies of how God is working in the lives of believers.

Because the Sunday Gathering isn't the draw into church, the focus and purpose and attention given toward the weekend changes from that of most Sunday focused churches. We spend less time focused on corporate gatherings. Sunday Gatherings are simple. They feel more sacred. They reflect what we read about in Scripture. The production value is low. The sanctity and sacredness and spirituality of the moment is high.

Generally, believers gathered weekly, regularly, when they were able. Sometimes, because of persecution, travel distance, or other difficulties, the individual House Churches would gather with other connected House Churches corporately, but less regularly.

Today, some Churches of House Churches corporately gather weekly, as they have the ability to do so with ease and availability of space. Some Churches of House Churches gather corporately monthly, as space, distance, persecution, or other factors inhibit the weekly gathering.

We'll discuss later on the use of space for Sunday Gatherings in the biblical, historical, and global church.

CHAPTER 8

DIVERSITY IN COMMUNITY

A *church is more than a homogenous* life stage group. A church is diverse. A church has different age groups, different ethnicities, different marital status, different places in their spiritual maturity, different socio economic status, different spiritual gifting and ministries. In a church there are married and single, rich and poor, unbeliever, new believer, immature believer, mature believer, different colors and cultures.

Groups can be homogenous, but not a church. No church is, or should be, monolithic. Can you imagine a whole church of people just like one another?

Yet within most churches, most groups and classes are homogenous. This certain age, this life stage, these specific similarities, this certain ministry, these unite us together. Most people only gather in true ongoing discipleship community with people who are similar to them. Many people have close friends in their church community who are in their same life stage, same socio-economic bracket, same color skin, and same spiritual maturity level. But, have little to no community beyond their personal similarities.

Diversity deepens discipleship. Diversity reflects the early church. Diversity represents the gospel. The gospel destroys divisions.

Having friends in church is awesome. We should. I have them. My kids have them. In fact, my best friends come from within the church.

But, when Scripture uses identifiers for the church, it speaks about church primarily as a family. We are a spiritual family. But most people in church only live in true community as similar friends, and not in diverse family. We may be in the same auditorium with people who are different than us, but most often not in deep diverse relationships.

It's harder to make family in a church community than it is to make friends. Again, assuming that we don't define community as sitting in the same large room with people, but living life together in living rooms and kitchens and conversations and connected in closeness.

Most churches are pretty good at creating friendships, but not as great at creating family. We create homogenous groups in Sunday School, homogenous groups in Small Groups. This is where our closest community is. It's not bad. I'm grateful for so much of what this accomplishes. It just does not accomplish the fullness of what God expressed as His desires and descriptions for His church.

Diversity is multi-layered. Diversity includes, but is much more than, racial diversity. To live in actual community with someone unlike you is not only unusual, it is unique, rare, and difficult for many. Community is difficult, but crucial. Diversity in community is even more difficult if we have a church structured toward life-stage affinity.

The church should have Generational Diversity.

> *"Teach the older women to...then they can urge the younger women to..." Titus 2:3-4*

The church should have Socioeconomic Diversity.

> *"Do you despise the church of God by humiliating those who have nothing?" I Corinthians 11:22*

I believe one of the most difficult expressions of diversity to live together in unity with is socioeconomic diversity.

The church should have Ethnic Diversity.

"There is neither Jew not Gentile...for you are all one in Christ Jesus" Galatians 3:28

The church should have Diversity of Spiritual Maturity.

"...Until we all reach unity in the faith and in the knowledge of the Son of God and become mature, attaining to the whole measure of the fullness of Christ." Ephesians 4:13

The church should have Diversity of Spiritual Gifting.

"If they were all one part, where would the body be? As it is, there are many parts, but one body." I Corinthians 12:19-20

A couple who had lived in our community for decades, and who was very wealthy, came to our church community and grafted their lives together in a House Church. I casually met them, though had not gotten to know them personally for some time.

One day, the wife asked to have a meeting with me. As we talked, she shared her perspective of their experience in this kind of church community. Though they loved people, they had never been in a community with people who were unlike them. Their community consisted of wealthy, successful, educated, same color skin, same general spiritual level of maturity, same generation, same stage of life, types of people.

They had never experienced diversity in community. Though they were very generous, they had never had biblical or personal discussions in kitchens or living rooms or around tables with people in their church who were not wealthy.

Though they studied the Bible regularly, they had never been in biblical or spiritual discussions with people in their church who had not grown up in the church, and who did not know a lot about the Bible.

They had lived decades in church, with diverse generations engaged in their churches, but they hadn't been in discipleship relationships with people other than those in their generation.

She shared her previous community life experiences with me. Then she shared how uncomfortable she was in this context, and how resistant she was to diversity together in community. But then, she told me that she could never go back. She had now tasted such a deeper and different texture of the church than she ever had before, and she couldn't settle for less ever again.

CHAPTER 9

MINISTRY PARTNERSHIPS

While we can't read Scripture without seeing House Church, and Corporate Gatherings, we also see meeting needs taking place. The church was an agent of meeting needs in their community. Jesus did this and taught this, the apostles followed suit, and the early church was beautiful about it.

Jesus was pretty clear about serving those in need. He said whatever we did to the least of these, we did to Him. He told His followers to feed the hungry, give water to the thirsty, care for the widow, the orphan, the prisoner, and the oppressed. He would feed people, heal people, counsel people, bring the disconnected into a spiritual family, and so much more.

Meeting needs is a biblical, historical, and global presence in the church.

Where does the act of meetings needs occur in the church? Is this a practice and responsibility for every individual? Does the church corporately have structure to support this function of a follower of Christ? Do we just pay certain people to do this, and our participation is our giving?

Absolutely, every believer should be carrying out the calling of personally meeting needs of others. We should be discipling people toward this end. Every person in our church should be hearing regularly in corporate gatherings, in House Church, and in one-on-one discipleship, about their gifts and how they should exercise them to build the body of Christ, and to meet the needs of others.

But, the church corporately should also be working together to address the needs in a city. An individual can do much. A House Church can do more. But a Church of House Churches can accomplish massive amounts of impact together in a city.

For many cities, there are existing gospel-centered and need-meeting ministries already happening. There is effectiveness, expertise, leadership, and infrastructure already in place with existing ministries that doesn't need to be re-created by a church.

A church, leading their people to partner with existing effective ministries, is a great stewardship. Rather than spend much time and much money stepping into a new arena, partnering with an existing ministry maximizes money, time, and leadership. Ultimately, this leads to great effectiveness, which is the goal anyway.

But sometimes, there are gaps in ministries in a city where a church needs to initiate the resolution. If there is a need in the city that isn't being addressed by an effective, gospel centered ministry, the church should engage its leadership to initiate work into this arena of ministry.

Centralized Ministry Partnerships support House Church

As discussed earlier, a House Church is a church. And churches are comprised of many different gifts and passions and callings. A House Church has diversity of ministries represented in each House Church.

Within a single House Church, some may be called to foster or adopt, or support those who are fostering and adopting. Some may be called to work with the homeless. Or the prisoner. Or pregnant unwed teenage moms. Or drilling water wells. Or caring for lonely widows and widowers in need.

A further beauty of a House Church is its diversity in ministry. The entire House Church benefits from seeing and hearing about all of the diversity of work that God is doing in and through the body in that House Church.

To support the diversity of ministry within each House Church, a simple centralized leadership can be a resource to coordinate all of the ministries represented within each House Church, and direct them to the partnership opportunities available.

Because the church works through Ministry Partnerships, and because the church is decentralized, and because corporate gatherings are simple, and especially because House Churches take care of the needs of one another, there are not many serving opportunities that need to be filled within the church itself.

We sometimes say the the Son of Man didn't die and rise again, save us, give us His Spirit, entrust us with spiritual gifts, so that we could say our ministry is selling bagels on Sundays or parking cars or handing out bulletins or opening doors. These things may have some value, but surely, God intended more for us with the death, burial, resurrection of His Son, and the indwelling of His Spirit.

Typically, the overwhelming amount of volunteer hours are directed toward supporting a service within a church one hour a week. As a result of less serving needs for the church to sustain itself, people are free to serve their community, rather than spend their limited volunteerism supporting the inside revolution of the Sunday service machine. In this applied ecclesiology, people are serving in a ministry that is meeting needs and sharing the gospel in their community.

Generally, to accomplish the serving value in the community, churches will have serving events. This is typically a special day, a couple of times a year, where people choose a project to be a part of. Good things are accomplished on this day. But in this approach, serving in the community isn't a part of that person's life in an ongoing way. They are not using their gifts regularly, or building relationships through their serving.

Beyond serving out in the community on a regular basis rather than serving inside the walls of the church primarily, through Ministry Partnerships, a person is now serving in their passions, and convictions, and calling. Rather than meeting a need to sustain a Sunday service, people are meeting needs in the community that they are passionate about, and using their gifts to fulfill their calling.

It's important to remember why we form Ministry Partnerships. Not only is it practical and effective, but it's purposeful. When we teach on this topic, we say to our church, "What is the difference between a humanitarian or social organization and a church?" The answer is that a church meets needs to share the gospel, which is exactly what we can do through Ministry Partnerships. At times, Jesus would share the gospel without meeting a need, but He would not meet a need without sharing the gospel (Matt. 9:1–8). He cared about people's immediate needs, but He was primarily concerned about their soul.

As a church, we're going to teach the gospel without meeting physical needs at times, but we're not going to meet a physical need without representing the gospel. We care deeply about all the needs in our community- body and soul- yet, we care even more deeply about spiritual and eternal needs. We should always do this with grace, love, and gentleness, and as we are representing Jesus when we serve, we want to speak about Him if the opportunity arises. We're always going to meet needs, but we always want our serving and sharing and giving to lead to an understanding of the gospel.

As the gospel is the ultimate goal, we only form Ministry Partnerships with others who share this gospel focus and priority.

Some of the principles that guide our approach to Ministry Partnerships are:

- Pray, wait, and seek the areas in which God is calling us to serve, or has already clearly called us to in Scripture.

- Start with low-hanging fruit in our local community— what are the most basic needs around us that are not yet fully met?

- Discover a local Ministry Partner in the areas we sense God's leading, that already has some momentum but needs more resources and volunteers.

- Discern other nations we can serve as well. Join people on the ground, who know the local climate and culture and who are already doing great work. Support them with money, people, trips, and encouragement.

- Look for ministries where you can make a significant impact, rather than those where the effort-to-results ratio may not be high. We like to find smaller to medium sized ministries who, if we partner with them, can go to the next level of effectiveness. And, our people will be able to make an impact and be involved with them personally. Aim for ministries in need of both volunteer service and financial contribution. We avoid just sending a check, without sending people to partner as well.

- Develop relationships with ministries you can partner with for a long period of time. Longevity has great payoffs, and the relationships that are built can lead to great things. We endeavor to partner with a ministry and have a committed liaison within our church for relationship, accountability, and effectiveness. A liaison is the leader of the ministry in your church, and they serve to connect your church and the ministry partner. This helps the partnership run smoothly and maintains the quality of the relationship.

- In short, we first decide the domain we are called to serve in. Second, we discover and vet the Ministry Partner who is right for us. And third, we commit to partner with sending people and finances, and we develop a liaison to lead the charge within our church.

One Saturday I was working at a house that cared for kids who had aged out of foster care. There were a lot of other people from our church there with me. The leader of that ministry created a moment where all of the people who served in that ministry on a regular basis were coming together for a big project. I heard about it, and wanted to join. It was also an opportunity for people who were considering engaging their life with that ministry could investigate this place and people and purpose.

I spent time working on a task with a man in our church who I have much love and respect for. He stopped working for a moment, and got emotional. I assumed his emotion was because of the hard stories we had heard of the incredibly difficult lives these kids have had to live on their own.

This man from our church told me that out of his decades of engagement in local churches for most of his life, this is the first time he was ever a part of a work day that wasn't at his local church building. He said that there would often be work days to clean up a church campus, and do projects on his church building. But, he had never served at any ministry beyond his own church campus. He was glad to be doing so today. And he was sad that he had never before.

CHAPTER 10

RADICAL GENEROSITY

A *fourth value of our church, that* we saw modeled through the early church, is radical generosity. This is related to our simplicity. Our language to express these biblical values is that we practice "Simplicity for the Sake of Generosity."

We started with a target that half of our budget goes outside of the walls of our church—to meet needs and plant churches. We planted with this intention. We are strategic in our systems and are reductionists in all we do.

We practice the principle of "Reduce and Refine" at the outset of any endeavor, and through the ongoing work we do as a church. We pay attention to this, especially in the largest costs related to our building and staff. I heard years ago that 98% of churches keep 97% of their offerings to work within their own walls, and most of that is spent on the church building, its staff, and inside programming. Most church budgets I have led, managed, or know of have been at or close to these numbers.

We cut in building costs because we keep our space simple (we discuss a theology and approach to space in the following chapter). We don't want to ever be in a position where we are compromising our values or biblical approaches in order to pay our bills.

Beyond distributed leadership and priesthood of the believers, generosity is another reason that we also minimize the size of our staff. Most churches our size have three or four times as many staff members as we do, but our structure and systems allow us to accomplish more with fewer people.

We constrain our spending by our commitment to radical generosity. The structure of our church feeds into our desire and calling to be radically generous. We are able to have less staff and simple space because of the structure of our House Churches and Ministry Partnerships.

For example, we don't need administrative assistants. Our staff is not central. Our building is not central. We are decentralized. We don't have a phone number for anyone to call, and no receptionist to answer our foyer or phones. And our programming is simple, reduced, different…we have Sunday Gatherings, House Churches, and Ministry Partnerships. And we have occasional life stage events connecting people across, and into, House Churches.

This means there are things people may have been used to doing in other churches that they won't find at Church Project. We often teach our ecclesiology so people understand the reasons behind our differences. Our difference from past places for re-churched people requires us to reshape people's thinking about what the church is and isn't, what programs it should and should not provide, and what pastors do and don't do. People have to take more initiative for our ecclesiological approach to work, but we find that many are willing to and wanting to. So, we teach what the Scriptures say about church, pastors, and people serving.

We read in Acts 2 that the believers in the early church met one another's needs. They sold their things and shared with anyone who had need. This happens throughout House Churches. Beyond our goal of corporate giving, we have no idea how to measure the massive amounts of generosity flowing through Church Project people to one another.

The early church met one another's needs. But, they also brought their money and laid it at the church leader's feet, submitting their giving to the leadership God placed over them. People bring their giving corporately to submit it to the leadership of the church, so that we can corporately do all that we need and are called to do- support our relatively small team of vocational pastors, pay our relatively smaller expenses, and give together to our ministry partnerships and church planting.

Beyond corporate offerings, the frontline of benevolence happens in the context of House Churches. Most churches I've worked in, if not every one of them, had a fairly bureaucratic process and budget for meeting others' needs. It was typical for a person in need to come into the office, fill out a form, and then meet with a person who gave leadership in the area of benevolence.

I remember once when a mother called the office and set up an appointment for financial help. Her husband had left their marriage and left her with the kids, and no support to pay the bills. She came into the office at the appointed time, filled out a form, and waited.

Soon, an executive pastor who she had never met came and welcomed her back to his office. She shared her story of brokenness and need. He was compassionate and kind, and began to ask all of the protocol questions, like, "How much do you make, and what's your debt, what are your plans, etc.?" He let her know that we could pay her mortgage for two months, but beyond that, the benevolence budget was limited, and we probably couldn't do more.

She walked away grateful for the help we gave, though a little embarrassed to expose her brokenness and personal financial situation to a stranger. But she would likely find herself only a couple of weeks away from being in the same situation again, and had now exhausted her church option.

That just doesn't seem like what I read about in the book of Acts. There, the church knew each other, recognized each other's needs, and lived in continuous community. They met each other's needs- even if they had to sell their own stuff to do it. The church was intimate, personal, pure, and costly. People sacrificed for one another! In the church of thousands, they met each other's needs through the community they lived in by the dozens. That type of generosity increases the commitment and intimacy of the church to one another.

Seeing this type of generosity in Scripture always excited me, and I wanted to see that happen in the church in our day! At Church Project, we have created a situation of sharing and generosity by removing a centralized structure, gathering people in community, and allowing the people to care for one another in House Churches. We see this happen all of the time. It's one of my favorite things about our church.

A husband and father in our church lost his job and was looking for work. He was weeks in between jobs, and couldn't pay his bills. The couple mentioned it at House Church because we are authentic, share our needs, and pray for one another. The next week when this couple came to House Church, there was a sack of money on the table. The group said, "We got together, took up money, and we're paying your rent for the next couple of months."

One House Church had somebody who needed a car because their car broke down, and they couldn't buy a new car to get to work and take their kids to school. Somebody just gave them a car.

Another House Church had an older single lady who had recently joined her life into a House Church, after she had just been fired from her job at another church. She started coming to our church shortly before she had a surgery—a life-altering surgery—that was going to bankrupt her. Within four weeks, her House Church raised almost exactly the significant amount of money that she needed. When they couldn't meet the total of all of the needs, the corporate giving of Church Project stepped in.

These few examples are a microcosm of the benevolent things happening in our House Churches. The stories are ongoing, uncountable, and sometimes almost unbelievable. I've never experienced anything like the generosity shared between believers in House Churches.

Another benefit of having needs met within a close community is that people know whether or not those in need are truly in need, or just being lazy and taking advantage of generosity. Paul encouraged the church in this fashion when he cautioned them to discern whether or not a widow was a "widow indeed" (1 Tim. 5:3–5). We believe those in a House Church, with guidance from their House Church pastor, are able to decipher between those who are truly in need and those who are not. But, we've had little to no experiences where people tried to take advantage of the generosity of a House Church. Intimate community is a detractor for deceit.

In terms of our church's corporate giving, God has called us to direct a comparatively large percentage of our corporate budget toward church planting and gospel centered ministries. Radical generosity has been one of our greatest joys, and probably our most difficult challenge. But, it has been a distinctive mark that has shaped our church from the outset.

I don't say any of this to elevate our generosity above others. I say it as an example of what can happen when the church prioritizes simplicity and generosity that mirrors what we see in the New Testament. At Church Project, we delight in being simple in order to be generous. Collectively, we have the power to really make a difference. If we keep it simple within the walls of our church, then we can give our money to many other things that will last eternally—meeting needs and sharing the gospel.

BIBLICAL.SIMPLE.RELEVANT.GENEROUS.

These four values drive everything we do, and once they were in place the other dominos began to fall. Our structure allows the pastors to do what God has called us to do: "Equip people to do the work of ministry" (Eph. 4:12). House Church pastors, Ministry Partnerships, a reduced and invisible central office, less programming- it all means fewer staff, more people being empowered for ministry, and more money freed up for Ministry Partnerships.

I remember our first global Ministry Partner who visited with us when we were about six months old as a church. We asked these friends what they needed, and they said they needed a van to get kids to church from a very poor village. We bought them a van on the spot.

One time, while visiting one of our Ministry Partners in another country, a couple of people from our church took an excursion with me to visit a potential site for a partnership with a school and church. The building where this school and church were meeting was almost collapsing on the kids. I asked them how much a new building would cost, though I knew the approximate amount because we had built other buildings in that country. The pastor told me an accurate number in the tens of thousands, and I told him he'd have the money in a week. We sent it to our partners on the ground, and they began construction immediately.

I met one local Ministry Partner very early on in our partnership. I asked him what he needed. His answer, "I need a truck to deliver our meals to the homeless." I asked him the price, and he said, "It's about $20,000 to buy it and get it ready to serve food." I said, "Okay, here's a check- our church will joyfully buy you the van. Thank you for all that you do."

When we met one of our now largest Ministry Partners, the leaders sat on our couch after their former church had just transitioned away from partnership with them. I asked them, "How did your last church partner with you financially?" I wanted to make sure they didn't have gaps left over from this church not continuing their support. They said, "They gave us $250, twice. And we are grateful for that." I said, "We're going to immediately do about 10 times that- every month. Then, we plan to increase that as we are able and meet other needs along the way as you have them. We're doing this so that you can lead your ministry into everything God has called you to do. We believe in you!" They got tears in their eyes because they were overwhelmed at the support. That ministry was already great, but we had the opportunity to partner with them to help the ministry go to other levels of impact. They're changing the world.

CHAPTER 11

THEOLOGY OF SPACE

Space is not sacred, but sacred things happen in space.

O ften, the word church is used for a building. The beautiful word that was intended to communicate the mystery in form of the body of Jesus, has been applied to bricks and concrete and steel and stuff, rather than to human beings radically rescued by Jesus.

"See you at the church. Don't run in church. When does the church open? I left something at church." All of these phrases and many more are used regularly to describe a place made up of materials.

This isn't so bad, unless we've conflated the understanding of the word church, with place. And sadly, this is often the case. For most understandings, church is a building. Rather than describing the people, the church is a place.

So, is place bad? Is space bad? (I interchangeably use the words space and place.) Should the church not meet together? Or should they not meet in a place? Or, should they only meet in a house as a place? Is a house exempt from negative place and space and somehow has some holiness attached to its humility?

I believe there is a theology of space. We have some theological view of the sacredness of space.

In the Old Testament, the gathering of believers was centralized in space. And that space was awesome! The temple! That place was sacred. People were in awe of that space, they wrote songs about that place. And other spaces were sacred. The tabernacle. The synagogue.

But then, Jesus said that temple would be destroyed. And also that His temple, His body, would be destroyed. And then, He said that upon our salvation and receiving of His Spirit, we were now the temple of the Holy Spirit.

So, the sacred space was gone. And now, our bodies are sacred. But, if we are to gather, we still need space (at least here in Houston we do! Mosquitos, sudden thunderstorms from the storehouses of hail, hot and humid as a rain forest for a third of the year...)

So if space is not bad, and we need a place if we are to gather, but space is not sacred, what do we do with space?

I have a saying to help our church reorient our theology of space and place. "Space is not sacred. But sacred things happen in space." Of course, you can use the word place, in place of space, if that helps you.

In American Christianity there is a residue of what I call "temple theology" in the church. There continues to be some semblance of sanctity to space. So rather than space being utilitarian where sacred things can occur, the space itself becomes sacred. The space itself is set apart as sacred. This works for the times when sacred things are happening here. But, this "sacred space theology" reduces the ability to have non-sacred activities occur in space. This is why most buildings are used only a few hours a week.

Because of a sacred space residual temple theology, some people only think that they are a church if they have space. And, the health and effectiveness and impact of some churches are gauged upon the beauty and size and strength of their space.

In the book of Acts, the believers were gathering by the thousands regularly for teaching and worship, but then got kicked out of the temple courts when the temple ruler converted and became a follower of Jesus. They continued gatherings by the thousands when they were ousted from the area, and moved next door, to a rented lecture hall, called Solomon's Colonnade.

Throughout the rest of the book of Acts we see different times where the church would be removed from the corporate place where all of the House Churches were using to gather together, and be disbursed to another place. It's surely something many churches deal with today.

There is an argument for owning space. But, it's a theological stretch to argue for owning sacred space.

When space is not sacred, it can be shared. When space is not sacred, it can be stewarded. If a Church of House Churches decides to own space, it should include the reasons of sharing the space, and stewarding the space.

If a Church of House Churches decides to own space, it should share the space. Many needs are happening in a city where shared space can be used for good of the city. Ministry Partners need space for training, meeting, offices, and more. Other churches need space for gatherings and events. Non-profits, schools, teams, and other ministry partners need space for practices, presentations, galas, and more.

Additionally, great things to serve the city can be used with the space. Artists in the city need a place to display their art, and a city-wide art exhibit (with some guiding parameters) could be a way the space could serve the city. Farmers and creators of goods need a space to sell and share their goods with the community, and a Farmer's Market kind of event can serve the city in this way.

Space can be shared. To share the space well, the space design should support not just sacred things, but should be space that lends itself to sharing.

Space can be stewarded. To steward the space well, the design should support not just sacred things, but the ways in which the space will be stewarded. Corporate events that can rent space, schools that need space to rent, city wide events that need space to rent, sporting events, etc., are examples of ways to use the space to steward financially, and leverage the resources for kingdom causes.

My first trip out of the country was on a mission trip to Mexico the summer after I graduated high school. I was in a little town a couple of hours south of the border of Texas, just a little into the interior. It affected my life in profound and enduring ways.

I remember going into this little church building that had no a/c. One room for all of the little kids. It was simple. And it worked for them. I remember thinking that this was essentially like we do here in our country, just on a much smaller and simpler scale.

Now, I've traveled to dozens of nations. I've been in gatherings in homes, in borrowed office buildings, in rented venue spaces, and in lean to's. I've been in buildings in some countries that I thought literally may collapse while we were in there if a gust of wind came through.

If space is sacred, then the wonderful worship of God isn't happening in most of the global places where I've been. Many of these places are less than sanitary, much less sacred spaces.

I love it when people walk into our building for a Sunday Gathering. They are curious about the space. Our church community bought a building. It's a huge old athletic facility that was shut down for several years because the owners didn't want to pour more money into it to replace the hurricane damaged hardcourt wood floors. We have concrete floors and plastic chairs. The place looks great, clean, contemporary. But, it doesn't look like a typical church building. Even our space is sending a message very quickly that this space is not sacred. But, also pretty quickly, anyone will know that we will be doing sacred things in this space during the time that you're here.

I have found that not having a "church" building- whatever that means, however that man-made not-from-the-Bible definition came about- is absolutely disarming to people who haven't been to a gathering of believers in a long time, or ever. I have also found that believers who love Jesus don't need a building to be "churchy". I admit, there is some nostalgia lost for me sometimes when I walk into different "church" buildings. I enjoy some of the feeling that the space exudes. But, when I wrestle with the Word, I see that these are philosophical luxuries only parts of the world can choose to justify. And theologically, we can't.

I'll also say here - don't throw this baby out with the bath water. We can disagree on things and still learn from each other. I have plenty of friends and other people that I respect who disagree on this and other matters. I would just ask you to bring your Bible when we have this respectful discussion!

CHAPTER 12

DISCIPLESHIP

Everything Jesus did was about discipleship.

J esus came to make the way for salvation and reveal the kingdom and call followers to Himself.

Jesus taught by the thousands on a mountainside to make disciples. He lived life together daily for 3 1/2 years with a dozen men to make disciples. He spent time with people one-on-one to make disciples. And, He met needs in order to make disciples. All of these things started an enduring global movement of making disciples.

Everything Jesus did was about discipleship. He called and commissioned us to make disciples. Everything we do as a church should be about discipleship.

Our Sunday Gatherings should be intentional about making disciples. Our House Churches should be intentional about making disciples. Our Ministry Partnerships should be intentional about making disciples. And, we should be intentionally making disciples in one-on-one relationships.

One-on-one Discipleship is "One Jesus follower leading another person to follow Jesus." People in relationships and conversation, rather than classes or curriculum, was Jesus's way of discipleship.

Because of Jesus's relational discipleship example, we want every point where people need to move forward in their relationship with Jesus and His church to happen personally, where possible, when we are in proximity to people. Not digitally. Or programatically. Or simple access to information. Or in large groups of information dissemination. But we ultimately want moving forward with Jesus and His church to happen through personal relationship and conversation and accountability.

We pursue developing people in every arena of our church in how to have personal discipleship conversations with people, and know how to help move them along as they pursue their relationship with Christ. We have people developed to have these conversations in our foyer before and after our corporate gatherings. We have people in every House Church developed with the intention of leading each person in their House Church to be discipled, then to disciple someone else. Every Ministry Partnership has leadership prepared to personally disciple everyone engaged in that specific ministry.

The larger a church gets, the more difficult it becomes to stay organic and personal and relational through processes. Many churches make decisions as they grow that compromise their original organic intentions, because scaling is much easier when it happens through digital systems, programs or classes. But, though more difficult, these approaches are less effective. And, we have now seen, it is possible to keep the origins of relationship present through processes even with thousands of people.

At Church Project, we struggled through this situation for some time. We had outgrown our original organic abilities of moving people personally through simple relational systems. But, we knew that we did not want to compromise our relational and organic essence by systematizing people digitally or programmatically. In our journey to discover a new way to ensure discipleship was continuing to happen through personal relationships, we remained faithful to our axiom that says, "we say no until we get to the right yes." We remained static in our growth for some time, not knowing how to accomplish one without compromising the other. At a point in our wrestling through these tensions, and being offered many solutions that would not fit our principles, God connected my path with a person who understood our values and ethos, and helped lead us into creating scaling systems that were personal and relational, and highly effective.

As any pastor should, there are many things I love about our church. But, one of the things I love the most is going into coffee shops or restaurants around our city, and seeing people there who are being discipled and discipling someone else. I'll see people having coffee, their Bibles open, talking, sometimes crying, praying for each other. It's beautiful.

We have many hundreds, maybe even thousands, of people that have been trained intentionally to know how to and be actively engaged in discipling another person. No classes. No curriculum. No program. Just relationships, and Scripture. Time with another person, intentional discussions based completely in the Word, teaching them how to follow and love Jesus, learning how to study the Scriptures for themselves, and developing them to be ready to do this with another person very soon.

One of the things that makes it so beautiful for me is knowing how they got connected. One of the people in the conversation was personally trained in how to disciple someone. And most probably, they were connected through their House Church. I know the general conversations they are having, the verses they are memorizing, and the topics they are covering. This is so crucial to our calling as a church, we have a pastor who works full time giving oversight and direction to this. He doesn't teach classes or write curriculum. He trains many people how to make disciples, and he places trained people in all arenas of our church.

I also know at some point soon in this discipleship relationship, the person who is being discipled will have been equipped, expected, and supported, to replicate this same process and relationship with someone else. It's built into our culture. It's who we are. We have some people who are several generations deep of disciples now. It's unending in its possibilities.

We want to multiply at every level.

We want every disciple to multiply into discipling someone else.

We want every House Church to multiply into planting another House Church.

We want every Church Project to plant another Church Project.

CHAPTER 13

LIFE STAGE
CONNECTING EVENTS

Life Stage Connecting Events support House Church.

Because of this ecclesiological structure, there are little to no programs in a church. Programs are often substitutes for more intimate community, or relational discipleship. People most often will default to the least invasive form of community or discipleship available to them.

People would often rather take a class, instead of an accountable personal one-on-one discipleship relationship. People would often rather be involved in a selective program of their choice, rather than live together closely in a diverse House Church committed community.

Events aren't programs. Events can't become substitutes for community or discipleship. Events don't last. And events don't perform the functions of personal discipleship relationships or House Church. However, occasional intentional events can start people in a direction for discipleship or community relationships.

There are events that can be beneficial to the body. Events do not sustain community, and events do not provide substitutes for community. Events can start some things that the fundamentals of this ecclesiological expression of church can't facilitate as easily when a church grows in numbers.

When a single mom comes into our church community, she needs a family. She'll graft into a House Church and have a support system of married and single people, younger and older, and people who will step in and help meet her needs. But, she also needs some friends who are just like her.

When this single mom comes into our church of 200 people, it will be easy to connect her with another single mom. For example, one single mom may be in House Church #3, while another is in House Church #5. When our church was smaller, we were generally able to organically connect people into friendships across different House Churches. We would see someone across the foyer, have a conversation, make an introduction, walk away, and a friendship would be starting behind us.

But, when you have 4000 people and 52 House Churches, how do you help single mom in House Church #2, connect with single mom in House Church #12, #22, #32, #42, #52, #62 and #72? You have a dinner. Or some event. Then they meet, they form friendships, and they carry those on beyond the event.

They return to their House Church for a strong, diverse, comprehensive family. But they can also set up their own movie night with their other single mom friends from many different House Churches.

The same scenario is true for almost every demographic as the church gets bigger. When your church gets to a size corporately that it is difficult to connect friendships of similar life stages organically throughout the multiplicity of House Churches, it may be time to consider initiating occasional life stage events. However, guard against the occasional events replacing the discipleship community that House Church provides. (Because people's past, and their proclivity, will automatically default toward homogenous community. But it's better that people have a diverse family of believers to support and disciple and care for one another, than a group of people who are just like one another.)

One example of our connecting events is an event we have for young married couples get to know other young married couples that are disbursed across many different House Churches. These young married couples spend a few weeks, before a Sunday Gathering, in someone's living room. They talk about marriage, are connected to a marriage mentor. And, we ensure they are engaged in a House Church. After a few weeks, they don't meet formally. But, young married couples who didn't know many other couples like them are now hosting dinners at their houses, going on trips together, etc. And, they're involved in a House Church, having community with a diverse family gathering around them, because the event is over, and not enduring as a possible replacement for diverse community.

I think there are several stages of life that can be the hardest to endure, and providing connection opportunities for these life stages can be an incredible gift to your church community.

One difficult life stage is after college, when someone has left the last real monolithic context for friendships they will ever have in life, and in one day go into a very diverse world where you often don't know anyone, and don't know how to know anyone.

Another difficult stage is when a couple is newly married. Transitions are happening, friendships and family relationships are changing, and people are figuring out how to be married.

Another difficult stage is stay-at-home moms. Many young moms talk about how lonely they are during this time. Not only is it difficult being a good mom, but it's difficult to be isolated away from other people going through similar struggles.

Another especially difficult stage of life is after someone goes through a divorce. Everything changes. Friendships change. Time with kids and time alone changes. People have free time that often they didn't want to have. People are going home to an empty house when they haven't done that in years. People are missing their kids, or taking care of their kids alone.

Another life stage that has proven to be difficult for many is being retired and elderly. This is true especially for unmarried elderly, though many married elderly still find this stage of life difficult. Often people are lonely, struggle through things alone, and are searching for their purpose and value.

Another difficult life-stage is being chronically ill. I've heard stories of loneliness from people who have dealt with chronic illnesses, that their life changed drastically, everything they had access to before has changed, and life is depressing.

Creating family is more difficult than creating friendships. A Church of House Churches will help create a spiritual family. Life stage events will help create friendships.

CHAPTER 14

FOURTH CENTURY ADJUSTMENTS AND RAMIFICATIONS

At some point, something shifted. It's not now what it originally was and was becoming. (But, it can again become what it was intended to be!)

What changed?

Centralization drastically increased. Place and priest replaced home and pastor.

A move was made to return to primary place, and primary priest. A dramatic mirror to the Old Testament priesthood and temple was being embraced again in the New Covenant. People went to a primary place, to a primary priest, to be their intermediary for all spiritual things.

The building became sacred once again. Jesus took the focus off of the temple, and onto the collective body of individuals. And at some point, the place where sacred things occurred returned to significance. The sacred space returned to be the place where the sacred things occurred.

In addition to sacred space, we once again had sacred people. Certain people were put into the place of the priest, alone qualified to administer the sacraments, teach the Scriptures, and pastor the people. The sacred priest in the sacred space was now the person who did all the priestly duties, very similar to the Old Testament priests - just without as much blood shed. The reinstitution of the sacred priest all but demolished the priesthood of the believer.

In lieu of priests, many have substituted sacred pastors. Though these sacred pastors would not claim to be an intermediary, many perspectives hold that many pastoral duties are reserved for people in these pastoral positions. Baptisms, funerals, weddings, counseling, benevolence, discipleship, accountability, oversight, decisions...these are often reserved for special pastors/clergy employed by the body. Duties reserved for priests only, are often also for pastors only, minus the confessions.

In lieu of temples, many have substituted sacred church buildings. Space is sacred. This is a church building. How we behave in this certain space is different than how we behave in other spaces. And, other things don't happen here. This space is sacred and set apart for sacred things only. One concern about this idea of sacred space, is that we can't find it in Scripture, or the first several centuries beyond the apostles.

The early church started with distributed leadership, priesthood of the believers, and sacred things happening in space, but space was not sacred. This carried on for several centuries. And, so did the rapid multiplication of the gospel. Followers of Jesus and churches planted were spreading around the world.

The fourth century Church changed the new church. Christianity became a name and a religion, and a social and political benefit. The state made the church a state church. The state used the church, and the church used the state. And the state church became centralized in special sacred buildings, and clergified with special sacred priests. The distribution and the power of pastoring was taken away from the priesthood of the believer. Movement slowed. And, where this centralization is present today, so is the slowness of movement. These two structural changes have been the major cause of the rapid decline of multiplication and movements.

As discussed in previous chapters and seen through Scriptural examples, some centrality is necessary for sustaining any multiplicity of leadership at even the local level. But, the greater the centrality, the slower the movement. When a church has to have enough sacred pastors to pastor the people, movement slows. When a church has to have a space that can be set apart as sacred, movement slows.

There is momentum within the church today that is returning to the first century practices of distribution of leadership, priesthood of the believer, and space that is not sacred, and decentralized away from central place and person and program.

CHAPTER 15

THE PURPOSE OF STAFF IN A CHURCH OF HOUSE CHURCHES

Most churches spend most of their money on their buildings and their staff.

I f you don't need sacred space, you can have simple space. Or shared space. Or steward space. And that saves a lot of money.

If you have House Church pastors as the front lines of leading and caring for all of the people in the church, you don't have to hire a ton of pastors to pastor the people. The people, the priesthood of the believer, are capable of that. Not hiring a pastor for every person saves a lot of money.

And if you spend less of your money on place and pastors, more money can be invested into other Kingdom causes. More money can be directed to church planting, and into Ministry Partnerships locally and globally.

So now, the pastors' roles are to "equip the saints for the works of ministry." If someone is going to steward money for a salary on behalf of their church, it is because the role requires so much time and attention that another vocation would be a distraction and a limitation to the work required.

In a Distributed leadership and Decentralized Diverse Discipleship community expression of church, a staff would exist to support these House Church leaders as they lead. Rather than staff pastors doing all of the work of ministry, now a staff pastor's role exists to help these leaders as they lead. And, paid staff help fill the few gaps created from this approach, like connecting people across and into the many Ministry Partnerships, connecting people across and into House Churches through life stage events, etc.

So, depending upon the size of the church, there may be no one paid by the church vocationally. If a church has a couple of House Churches, there may be no need yet to have any paid staff. But, if there becomes oversight of many House Churches, there will be roles that demand so much attention that the ministry demands require vocational attention.

Bi-vocational roles are often possible. But sometimes a full time staff position is needed. If not willing to pay someone when scaling happens, the person overseeing and supporting the many leaders will be working a full time marketplace job for money to live, and also working beyond a reasonable amount of hours for the church community. This is neither healthy nor honoring.

The main points of centralization in a Church of House Churches are elders, Sunday Gatherings, and Staff who support. We try to follow the model of Paul, working marketplace when necessary and possible, but working fully vocationally on ministry when needed and able. Paul also sent leaders that he had been developing (Titus, Tychicus, Crescens, etc.) to lead in churches where he saw the greatest needs for a pastor or overseer.

We have a very small staff compared to other churches our size. Our goal is a golf score, keeping the paid staff size as low as possible. We want to also maintain health on our staff team and throughout our church, especially support for those Decentralized Distributed pastoral leaders who are pastoring House Churches and leading Ministry Partnerships in our city.

We have a small team that focus only on House Church. Every House Church pastor and host has a pastor overseeing them. For example, one person on our staff pastors over 20 House Churches, supporting the pastors and spouses and hosts, meeting with most or all of them several times a month, essentially discipling them, developing them, watching over them, encouraging and caring for them, and pressing into cautions and concerns.

We have a small team that oversee our ministries to kids and students and their parents. We want kids and students to have friends in church that cross over many different House Churches. And, there are specific needs kids and students have, and opportunities to support parents.

We have a small team that oversees our corporate gatherings and anything that we do online. These are technical skills, and require more unique gifts and development and time than I would have anticipated before engaging these ministry areas.

We have a small team that oversee all of our finances. We want to make sure we are above reproach in anything that we touch concerning giving toward the kingdom.

We have a very small team - one for local, and one for global - that oversee all of the support to our Ministry Partners. These two pastors also oversee House Churches bridging entry opportunities for thousands of people to engage in local and global ministries.

We constrain our hiring by our commitment to generosity, distribution of leadership, and decentralization away from place and priest.

Also, our staff team is fairly invisible. There's no foyer or receptionist. No one knows where someone offices. There is no phone number to call. No staff names or pictures or emails are on our website. We remove the ability to circumvent House Church, and we protect our small staff from getting overwhelmed by being pulled into the front lines for pastoring our church. We are not equipped for that. We facilitate a Church of House Churches. Everything flows through House Church, and exists to support House Church.

NECESSARY INITIAL NEXT STEPS WHEN ADJUSTING TO BECOME A CHURCH OF HOUSE CHURCHES:

Diversify Communities
Distribute Pastoral Leadership
Decentralize Away From Place and Clergy and Programs

FIND OUT MORE THROUGH:

www.churchproject.org
www.churchprojectnetwork.com
www.housechurchnetwork.com
www.housechurchconference.org

ADDENDUM 1
11 OF THE FIRST THINGS
I TELL CHURCH PLANTERS

Church has complexity because it is a body made up of so many different parts and systems. But a body is also simple- it is created and didn't create itself, it evolves, it works, and it runs autonomically with the right care and health. The complexity of pastoral ministry can't be discussed briefly, but I've learned a few things about the basics of church planting. If I could only have one quick conversation with a church planter, I would say some of these things:

1. Grab a team of pastors quickly. Find one or two people willing to risk it all with you, and treat them like the staff you hope for them to become. House Church oversight, Sunday Gathering leadership, and caring for families with Kids and Students is most important when starting a church. If you're limited in the amount of staff you can hire, people you can employ, or people you can even find to lead, find volunteers in these arenas first. The person who plants the church will most likely be teaching and overseeing House Church pastors initially, anyway, and from there you can begin to raise up more leaders.

2. Build a leadership team of the wisest counsel you can find at the outset. Wise counsel will protect you. You don't know enough to do this alone without the input from others. Having a plurality of leaders will comfort your church. Let the church know you have this team. They'll be glad to know that wise people are speaking into the church they are trusting their lives to. Find a variety of counsel. Aim high, and be specific with the request (tenure/role). Invite them into your decisions

and use them to help shape your actions. You'll need different perspectives.

3. Find a space to meet. Philosophically and theologically, the church has no limitations, but everyone is always in an actual place. Buildings are amoral. Don't make them immoral by exalting them or by attributing evil to them. Find the best, available, practical, affordable space that is one step ahead of your current needs. Not ideal is ideal. Not ideal will set a culture of gratitude, will keep the focus on the main things, and will instill an ethic of simplicity. Ideal will create entitlement. Use living rooms, parks, warehouses, rented space.

4. Set a schedule. The philosophy of church—your ecclesiology—is actually fleshed out in time and space. Heaven is timeless. Here is not. When do you do what you believe you should do? And practically, does this work for real people? What will you do when you gather, and how will it look? These are things you must decide ahead of planting.

5. Base your budget on what you have, not on what you hope to have. Wisdom is from God, as well as faith. It's not ungodly or unbiblical to be wise. You can't believe your way into money. You can pray for it and please God with what He entrusts to you, but you have to make decisions based on what you actually have.

6. Know who you are and don't change. You are planting this church because God called you to. If that's not true, get off of the plane before it takes off. And, make sure you're on the right plane. Make sure that this calling is from God and lines up with Scripture. If so, keep after it. Be super clear on who you are, what you'll be doing, and how you'll do it. Every change is an admission of ignorance, and people are aware of that. People will allow some of this, but not much. Change will always cost you. It will cost you time. It will cost you money. It will cost you energy. It will cost you trust. Every redirection takes

a hit on momentum and leader energy—communication, more communication, recommunication—then you lose people's trust because they don't know if you're going to change again.

7. Simplicity is difficult, but simplicity will save you. The younger and smaller you are as a church, the less you need to do. Major on the things that matter most. Do only those primary things with your time, money, and leadership. For us it was Sunday Gatherings, House Churches, and Ministry Partnerships. We did nothing else, and continually pressed into the health of these areas. That was our flywheel.

8. Always say no, and occasionally break this rule. Everyone will have an idea, suggestion, passion, and vision, but their thoughts might end up wrecking your calling and dreams. It's a good sign that they have ideas (it means they care), but you need to know how you'll respond beforehand. I had phrases that helped as responses to requests and suggestion: Say thank you, say no, say why, say no, say thank you. People will always have ideas, convictions, and passions that do not line up with what your leadership wants to do or where it wants to go. We have to treat people with grace, dignity, and gratitude, but we have to realize that not everyone is leading in the same direction as the church. When people make suggestions, we often say something like, "Thank you for caring about this church enough to share your idea with us, but we will not be able to do that, and here's why. (It will change our schedule, our budget, our direction—whatever it may be.) So, we're not going to do that, but I'm very thankful that you care enough to suggest this." Don't just tell somebody no, but especially don't tell somebody maybe. "Maybe" leads to disappointment that can linger and build over time. Have courage to be kind, clear, and honest.

9. You can't be a pastor if you can't take a punch—get tough quick. You'll be sanctified in this arena more deeply than you think you'll need to be, and definitely more than you'll want to be. There are great, great people who will fight for you, and there are great people who will end up hurting you. You'll get punched and sucker punched. Every pastor deals with it. It's not personal to only you. I don't know a pastor who hasn't been hurt by people. Broken people will do hurtful things. You may actually hurt people too. It's no fun hurting people, or being hurt by people. Hurting people may be worse. Hopefully, you'll minimize this.

10. Don't shortcut integrity. The opportunities to shortcut integrity will come in many conversations and in a myriad of little decisions. The foundation of your church will be built on the integrity of your decisions and behavior.

11. You'll quickly discover how much you depend on the power of the Spirit and the power of the Scriptures. A church cannot be birthed and grow and be powerful without the supernatural intervention of God. And, the Scriptures that the Spirit wrote for us are more powerful than any words that any of us could craft on our own. So, depend on the Spirit. And, teach the Scriptures.

This list is by no means exhaustive—any church planter has stories from the trenches and wisdom to give. But, these eleven truths were essential aspects of what God showed me as I walked through the tough work of church planting, and I hope it will be useful to you as well.

ADDENDUM 2
THINGS THAT HAVE SURPRISED ME

Here are a few things that have surprised me in ministry, and have taught me that I'll never stop being surprised.

1. There will never be enough money. The vision will always precede provision. The provision will always fulfill the God-given vision—including its timing. If there is enough money, I'm not giving enough away. God uses limited resources to cause us to tighten our spending and depend on Him.

2. Leadership is a bigger challenge than it should be. Leading staff is tougher than you think it should be. Leading volunteer leaders is sometimes easier than leading staff. If I'm stewarding the church's offering to employ someone on behalf of the church, I would expect that the staff person's excellence, passion, and commitment to be higher even than our greatest volunteers. But this is not always the case. Also, leadership can be scary. The scary thing about being the leader is that you cannot hide. People know your strengths and weaknesses—you don't have to tell them. There has to be an inherent humility in accepting that you have areas in which you need to grow. And, if I don't have vision, no one will. Regardless of the great leaders around me, and regardless of the collective buy in to the calling, I have to lead forward.

3. You'll be more committed to this church than anyone else. I created an axiom— "In order to justify, people will vilify." People will justify leaving for reasons you would never consider. And, if people want to leave, they'll find a reason on which to base their decision. You don't have to agree or accept it, but that really doesn't

matter. People will leave more easily than you think they would. People will leave you though you've never left them. Some people can't stay—they don't have the capacity to work through things. It will bother you more than you'd think it would and more than it should. It will cripple your ministry if you don't get to a point of acceptance and peace. This has been my toughest challenge, biggest prayer, and greatest point of growth.

4. I've struggled with myself more than I could have dreamed I would. I often say that I needed so much sanctification, God made me a husband, a father, and a pastor. My biggest battle in pastoring and church planting is myself. Everything in and about me has been tested: My ambition vs. my vision. My never being satisfied vs. my passion and drive. My trust in the power and work of the Spirit vs. my trust in my own strength. My dependence on the Scriptures vs. my own cleverness. My peace and confidence vs. my identity in the "success" of my church. My belief in how much God loves me, sees me, and is for me. My commitment to my church and my belief in my calling. My insecurities. My faith in the work of God and His ability to do things. My marriage. My commitment to my family... This list could be much longer. I've learned so much, and I'm still learning. Every time I think I could not be surprised, I'm reminded that I'm very far from finished. Be encouraged that our very essence as pastors is to help people grow and shepherd them. But we are also sheep, and lists like this one are evidence that we're growing too. We are pastors; our work is to help people grow, to shepherd them. But we are also Christians, and our work is to yield ourselves to God's shepherding work in our lives. As a pastor, you'll always be learning, and you'll always be growing. It will always be painful. But growth is a sign of life, so be encouraged in the growing pains—and keep going and growing!

5. It is hard to start a church. It's even harder to stay. I started in 2010. It was hard. But twelve years in, it's been really hard to stay. I'm not sure which is harder. Honestly, I will say that if I hadn't started this church, I might not have stayed. I've had three or four seasons where I thought I might leave, I thought I couldn't stay. It's been an extra hard season for pastors through the pandemic, but other seasons were hard too. So, starting the church has probably given me different insight and love and level of commitment to this place and these people. Some seasons are for sure harder than others, some seasons are more fun or fruitful than others, But, I don't know a season that's not hard. There is always beauty in every season. Starting a church is hard. Staying is even harder.

ADDENDUM 3
VALUES OVER VISION

Church Project has tirelessly sought to mimic what we see in Scripture. However, we also wanted to make sure we approached these components in the spirit of the New Testament. That is, we wanted to discover what biblical values seemed to be at the heart of Jesus's ministry and the life of the early church.

I often suggest to church planters to be guided by their values rather than their vision. Our values guide everything we do. Vision is, of course, important. But, vision is often intangible and hard to measure. We actually don't know along the way how things will change, or if our vision and dream will be accomplished. People can get tired of waiting for the grand vision to ever be accomplished—the great and grand vision that they originally bought into didn't materialize like they thought it would, or soon enough. Vision can get exhausting while in pursuit of accomplishing it. And, the vision may never come to fruition.

But values always exist. Values can be practiced with 40, or 400, or 4,000 people. Practice the same values, and the same structure, from the very beginning.

We know whether or not we have embodied our values. Values are seen immediately and continually. We expressed our values when we had 40, 400, or 4,000 people as part of our body. We have always been biblical, simple, relevant, and generous at every size and stage.

Also, you'll be known by your values more than your vision. When people come to our church, they mention our values, not our vision. People immediately know who we are, not what we're hoping to be one day. They say, "I love how biblical you are and that you teach from the Scriptures," or, "I love how simple it is here," or, "It's easy to understand the teaching," or, "I love how generous we are as a church."

Vision can change, or even not be accomplished. But our values don't change, and they're constantly present. They're part of our DNA. Generosity is part of who we are. Simplicity is part of who we are. We coined a phrase that says "Simplicity for the Sake of Generosity," which incorporates two of our guiding values. People remember and quote and love these values that they participate in.

Biblicity (I'm creating this word) is part of who we are. We believe the Scriptures are inspired and helpful and powerful today. We unashamedly teach the Scriptures.

Relevance is part of who we are. Relevance meaning understandable to all, not some sense of cultural coolness. Jesus could be understood by a priest and prostitute in the same conversation.

Not every church will have the exact same values (though, I would say all biblical churches should embrace many of the same values). But, we can all make sure that the values that matter most are embedded in our DNA, and seek to drive the church's mission by those values.

We wanted these values to drive our Gatherings, House Churches, and Ministry Partnerships. There are of course many values we follow, pursuing the heart and life and teachings of Christ. But, we expressed four values that would serve as the foundation and motivation of everything we do as a church, and would seem to be comprehensive points by which all other values would flow.

As a people, we would be unashamedly biblical, irreducibly simple, understandably relevant, and radically generous.

Unashamedly Biblical

The Word of God is the driving force of all we do at Church Project. We seek to mirror the biblical expressions of church we see in Scripture, and we spend time in the Word when we are together—both in our gatherings and in our House Churches. We're not ashamed to talk about whatever themes the Bible addresses. Teaching through books of the Bible forces us to do just that. Teaching in this fashion constrains us to discuss whatever God wanted us to know when He intentionally put His words in his Word. Sadly, it's undeniable that many churches today claim to be a church but their teachings are not based on the Word. For us, we have deep convictions that the Word must be our guide. In Colossians 1:24, Paul says, "I'm here to give you the Word in its fullness." Paul also told Timothy to "preach the Word" (2 Tim. 4:2). Everything we do must have the Word in it. We teach out of the Word, we exposit the Word, and we draw application from the Word. Our goal is to give our church the Word, rather than primarily teach our own creative ideas.

As pastors and preachers, not only are we teaching people the Word, but we are teaching people how to teach themselves the Word. So, we want people to daily study through books of the Bible so that they will learn the whole counsel of Scripture. But occasionally, people need the Bible to specifically address topics they are dealing with. That's why we occasionally teach topically—so that we can teach people how to be biblically accurate while still being topical. I'll often teach our people that my job is to expose and explain the Scriptures. Then, their job is to approve that it is true based on the Word, accept it as God's Word, and then apply it to their lives. Our Sunday gatherings, House Churches, and our one-on-one discipleship—all are based on the Word. We believe that the Word of God grows the people of God, so we center our ministry on the Word as much as possible.

Irreducibly Simple

The second defining value for our church, one that has become a hallmark of Church Project, is that we are irreducibly simple. We intentionally avoid designing our church around an attractional model that so often obscures Jesus. We think the person of Jesus is attractive on His own and doesn't need to be dressed up, covered up, or apologized for.

From our first days as a church, we didn't want to depend on anything attractive or attractional—from the place we gathered to the way we presented everything—and we still don't, because we don't want to distract from the purity of the gospel. Our understanding of not being attractive comes partly from the view the prophet Isaiah paints of Jesus in chapter 53:2: "He had no beauty or majesty to attract us to Him, nothing in His appearance that we should desire Him." God intentionally came to earth in the form of a man whose appearance people weren't attracted to. In fact, there was nothing physical about Him that we would be attracted to.

Maybe that's what God intended when He knit his Son together in the womb, and the Father intentionally designed Him to not be physically attractive. The body of Christ should look like Jesus, so we've been intentionally unattractive to resemble Jesus. Jesus was simple. His life and ministry—the way He lived and the way He went about making disciples—were irreducibly simple. I think Jesus was clean. I think He washed his clothes, brushed His teeth and hair, and had good manners. He was kind and a gentleman. He was educated and intelligent. But He wasn't attractive. He wasn't flashy or fancy. He could have been attractive if He wanted to. There was nothing about Him that was attractive, that would cause anyone to be drawn to Him by His appearance. I'm very convicted that we shouldn't do anything in our church's style, structure, or presentations to draw people to Jesus—other than display the gospel. If Jesus did not use attractiveness to draw people to Himself, if the sovereign God designed Himself in the flesh to not be attractive to people by His appearance, we should follow. Whatever methods Jesus did and didn't use are our guide and boundaries.

Jesus modeled this simplicity in His ministry, and so did the early church. In fact, around Church Project we often employ hypothetical conversations from the early church as a means of filtering our decision-making process. I'll assess decisions by wondering, "Would the early church fathers have this discussion? Would they be concerned about this?" I think often they would (or maybe they are?) wonder why we are discussing such things, focusing on such things, spending our time, money, energy, and prayers on things that are so far from what they did, and what they saw Jesus do. Perhaps they would be pleading with us to get back to the simplicity of the gospel and community, and preaching and teaching the Word, and serving one another, and being generous.

We think that doing church with irreducible simplicity uncovers Jesus. It removes the makeup and the dress, and it just allows Jesus to be seen as He is. So, how does that play out practically? For one, our appearance is different from many churches. Our appearance of our building, the way we dress, our handouts—all that we do is simple. We do not desire to impress people based on their attraction to lesser things. We deeply desire that the lost be saved, but we're not seeking approval of people. We're letting the gospel itself do that work. The Spirit attracts people to God, and the gospel is the power that saves them, not our beautiful, polished models or strategies.

To be clear, we're not intentionally repelling people. We love and want people. We care deeply about kindness, hospitality, and clarity. We're clean and clear. Everything about our building is simple. We began in an old warehouse, next we gathered in a former grocery store, and next a renovated athletic facility. We have unfinished floors and plastic chairs. We have no moving lights or fog or anything like that. Everything is simple—our handouts are simple, our worship gathering elements are simple, and our sermon is simple. One guy who works with us now, who previously spent 25 years traveling and preaching to hundreds of thousands of people with great effectiveness, told me, "You have the un-sermon sermon." We just exposit the Word and don't make a show of it. I've worked hard to make sure my eloquence or creativity or humor or ingenuity isn't the focus of the conversation when someone walks away. I want to teach effectively, and I prepare, pray, and study to do so, but I'm not trying to impress people with my sermon.

These are the kinds of things that make us different in the arena of simplicity. Jesus commanded the church to "make disciples" and "feed my sheep." That's really what we're called to do. If what we're doing isn't directly helping people become disciples, then we should not need to do it. He didn't. People will always express that everything has some ancillary benefit for discipleship, but at the end of the day we want to have direct impact on discipleship. That's why we are very committed to simplicity.

Understandably Relevant

We are committed to being understandably relevant to all people. Jesus is our model, and He was able to speak to the priest and the prostitute in such a way that they both understood Him. We want to make sure we're not taking our theological ideas and giving them to people in a way they can't grasp. My 30 years of studying the Bible, and my master's and doctoral seminary nomenclature aren't necessarily going to help someone understand God more. Those without the Spirit of God cannot understand the deep things of the Spirit, anyway, regardless of what words we use (1 Cor. 2:14). Even among Christians, Paul wanted to teach people deeper things, but they could not yet understand them (1 Cor. 3:1–2).

We don't want to hide truth from people—we want truth revealed to them, which comes by the Spirit of God at work in the hearts of the people. Our role is to make the language and presentation clear and compelling for all to see, and then trust God to do a work in people's hearts. In our church, we have seminary professors and we have homeless drug addicts, and we want to make sure both of them feel like they're hearing from God, understanding the Word, and being challenged and encouraged.

Furthermore, our methodology is simple and understandable to outsiders. We explain what we do and why we do it each week. We avoid unnecessary traditions that may be unusual for people. We explain things that people may not understand—from meditation, to studying the Scriptures, to communion, to the songs we sing. We've done everything we can to remove traditions and language that are not necessary and extra biblical and that can hinder someone from understanding the good news. At the end of our gathering, we have an avenue for those who want to pray with someone or talk about Jesus, and we clearly explain what happens there.

I believe that if an unbeliever gets the courage to walk into a church gathering, they're expecting to experience something different and deeply spiritual, so we should not be ashamed of who we are or what we do. But we should work to make that experience clear and understandable in non-religious language.

So, we are spiritual, but not confusing or cryptic. We've intentionally removed any veneer of superficial or confusing religion from our gatherings, and have just made it a place to seek God and understand Him more.

Made in the USA
Monee, IL
23 February 2024

53512799R00069